MY LIFE IN TRAVEL

MY LIFE IN TRAVEL

Letters To My Three Grandsons

Prof. Anthony S. Travis

To order additional copies of this book, contact:
Xlibris Corporation
0-800-644-6988
www.xlibrispublishing.co.uk
Orders@xlibrispublishing.co.uk
306462

CONTENTS

DEDICATION

This book is for the three boys, who are my grandsons, namely:

Stuart, Edward, and Samuel—May the world be gentle with them, and may they be as stimulated and as rewarded as I have been in my life, spread—as it has been—across this precious planet.

It is dedicated to four notable planners and friends, who are no longer with us, and who did not write their own rich personal stories. They are:

Bob (Professor Sir Robert) Grieve, The first Chairman of the Highlands and Islands Development Board, who did so much for Scottish Planning;

David Hall, a dedicated past Director of The Town & Country Planning Association;

John Davidson, the pioneer of the U.K. Groundwork movement, and contributor to so much in U.K. conservation, and

Jan-Krzysztof Buczynski, planner, architect, inspirational man, and friend for over 50 years.

I also wish to thank the staff of the CAPD Unit at the Queen Elizabeth University Hospital, Birmingham, whose continuous help during this past year and a half on Peritoneal Dialysis has enabled the writing of this book. I thank them, and bless them for it.

INTRODUCTION

I recently celebrated my 80th birthday, and at the big event, which was spread over a whole weekend, addressed my main speech to two of my three grandsons, who were present. One was away visiting his American relations in Boston, Massachusetts. After that memorable weekend, some friends suggested that I should expand upon my remarks made to my grandchildren at that event. Later, another friend suggested that with my rich life's experiences and travel plus the extraordinary family history, I should perhaps record it for the benefit of my three grandchildren, and there may even be some aspects which others may find of interest as well.

The events of my life have been split between several countries in which I have lived or spent periods of time. These are Wales, New Zealand, England, Austria, Scotland, the USA, and Poland, amongst them. The places in which I have worked during my life have ranged from Detroit and Delft, to Birmingham and Warsaw, from the Maldives and Edinburgh, to Hong Kong and Ashkelon, from the San Francisco Bay area, and Salzburg, to the Algerian mid-Sahara Desert. Thus my range of places and events experienced and of extraordinary people met, have been richly thought-provoking: it may thus interest some people beyond a scattered group of family and friends. Life has for me been in a "global village."

For long I have made up stories or fairy tales for my three grandsons, whose ages now range from 8 to 17. This story-telling book is for them, and possibly for others. It is a set of true stories, which I hope will interest, inform, and encourage them in the lives which face them, in this increasingly confusing, crowded, and rather troubled world.

ACKNOWLEDGMENTS

I would like to thank the following people for their help, criticisms, and suggestions during the writing and editing of this book:

- **Professor Valerie Sanders of Hull University's English Department, for her comments and positive encouragement**
- **My wife Philippa, and my daughter Abigail for their helpful remarks.**
- **Sincere thanks go to my friend of long standing—Michael Dower, for his meticulous and rigorous editing of the planning chapters, his informed criticisms, and constructive suggestions. Whilst we differ in our evaluations of the work of Sir Patrick Abercrombie, I cannot dissent from his view of that Scot's central importance in the historical development of professional planning practice in the UK, Ethiopia, and in British Mandatory Palestine.**

I wish to thank Nick Maslen Photography for the valued work he did on the photos.

CHAPTER ONE

A Designer helps the Empire in Two World Wars

The first story which I want to tell you is an extraordinary one of a man who travelled from across the seas—first to this country, later to the United States, and then from here, all the way to New Zealand. It encompasses a life in at least four countries. In the process, he was contributing—as a designer, to very important things that helped Britain in the 1st World War, and the Australasian part of the British Commonwealth, or Empire, in the 2nd World War.

Grandpa Michael Tavrogis was born in 1876 in Warsaw. He came from a very lively and loving family, I suppose it would be described as middle-class, as they comprised builders, architects, fashion-designers, leather tanners, and cabinet makers. They lived a long way away from here, in two cities. They were urban people living in two big cities, but in a rather difficult time, as the cities were Warsaw and Lodz in what was, in the late 19th Century, Czarist Poland! These cities were on the fringes of the great Czarist Empire that stretched from Poland, through to the far end of Siberia—facing Japan. This empire was subject to the whims and difficult decisions of

---

a remote and cruel Czar who sat in the Kremlin, and made autocratic decisions affecting scattered peoples over his vast empire.

What changed my grandpa's life was the fact that he grew-up with an extraordinary feeling for design in wood, but was growing up in a city which was subject to Czarist conscription. That was a form of conscription that took young men away from their families, who never saw them again, for the rest of their lives—because in the Czarist army they could be sent into the icy wastes of Siberia, to the remote port of Vladivostok, or to the desert wastes of Turkmenistan. Thus middle-class families fought hard to prevent losing their sons to this empire of a wicked Czar.

In 1897, aged 21, Grandpa Michael Tavrogis (a Spanish/ Portuguese surname!) married a beautiful young, 19 year old woman, called Hannah Kaczor, who came from the same city, but whose family was from Lodz. She was both a very talented and adaptable person. A few years ago, I learned that 'Kaczor' was the Polish word for 'Duck,' and was amused to think that my grandpa married "Miss Duck!" Hannah came to be known as 'Annie' through most of her life. Married at this difficult time and place, the big problem was how to enable their lives together to continue, by preventing Michael from being conscripted into the Czarist army, and being taken away forever from his new young wife, and wider family.

Surprisingly, a doctor was called to damage one of Michael's ear-drums, so that he would be unfit for military service. Nevertheless, he passed his medical. Under dangerous circumstances, the newly-married young couple fled from Warsaw, got over land either to Danzig—the free port on the Baltic, in the North of Poland, or to the Port of Hamburg in Germany. Thus they were able to come across to settle in England, as refugees from the Czarist regime. They came and set up home in 1897 in a strange and unlikely place, that was then the village of Edmonton, north of London, but not yet connected to it. In this village they settled down, and were to give birth to and bring up a family of four English-born sons—Morris, Jack, Harold (Harry), and Joshua (Joss). The first of two boys, who were born in Edmonton—were Morris, who was born in 1898, and then Jack, born a year later there, in 1898.

Grandpa Michael in the early 1900's
as a young migrant in England.

Grandpa at De Havilland's, New Zealand, with Lady Newall,
wife of the Governor General, in 1944.

This all took place in the late 19th Century, and I've still been unable to find out what work it was that Grandpa was able to do in this village, which later was to be connected by early tram cars into London. I do know that the elder son—my father—Morris—played in the church graveyard in Edmonton village, and that there he did his first explorations of life in this new land. Morris, born in England, was an extraordinary man, about whom I'll tell you later. What became clear was that early in the 20th Century, Grandpa Michael found it difficult to find suitable work in or near London. For some extraordinary reason, they went first to Leeds, where the two other boys were born, then decided to go to California, where he heard that there were work—opportunities for designers!

Thus it seems that Grandpa Michael took my grandma (and I assume those children who were already born!) across the sea to North America. Next they went across that vast continent by steam train, to this new part of American society—California. There, in 1904, a series of scattered new communities were growing up, and they moved to a small village where they first of all moved into an adobe, or baked—mud house. Such stock were available, because these were the sort of homes built in the Spanish tradition, in which the early settlers of California lived.

There he managed to get a job as a designer & maker of railroad carriages for the Santa Fe Railroad Company. It was building the rolling-stock for the trains, which were to travel over the new lines being constructed in California! The trans-continental rail-line had only been completed later in the 19th Century, and that linked the West of the United States right through to the East Coast.

I have only seen one photo of the second house which they lived in this village in California, and that was an early version of what we would now call 'a ranch-style house'. It was located on a small street, Jackson St., which was the main street of this settlement. It had one tram-car (or street-car), going up and down it. I remember many years ago asking my Grandpa about this place, and he said "Well in those days they called it in Spanish—'Los Angeles', long before it became known as L.A.!" It was a difficult place in which to live; it was very hot and dry, and apparently my grandma had heart problems. She found it hard to live there, because these were days long before air-conditioning was invented, and it was not easy to live under these harsh conditions in California. Thus it seems, because of her poor health, and for no other reasons, they came back to the UK, and returned to Leeds in Yorkshire, though, as far as I know, they had few links of any sort—there.

Looking at early photos of grandpa, you can see that he was a striking figure, of medium height, with a walrus moustache, clean-shaven, but a chain smoker of cigarettes, with nicotine-stained fingers, from a young age. At work, he always dressed in pullovers, shirts, and greys, always concentrating and immersed in whatever challenging task was in hand. His design work obsession led his wife to calling him "wooden head" or "blockhead!"—not because of stupidity, but because of his fixation with one material, namely wood! However, when he did take part in social events, grandpa always cut a striking figure—in his suits, and waist-coats, always adorned with his gold watch and chain. As grandpa lived with us till I was 18, he was someone whom I knew very well.

Grandma, in early photos, gives two contrasting impressions; one, when dressed up, of the Victorian 'Grande Dame' in her splendid, bejewelled, flowing, black silk gown, and huge ostrich-feather crowned hat. When in working mode, however, with rolled-up sleeves, and folded arms, she reminds one of 'tugboat Annie!'. Sadly, I never met this grandma, as she died years before I was born.

Grandma Hannah, dressed as a "Grande Dame" in London, early 1900's.

After being there in Leeds for a few years, Grandpa at last found skilled employment in what I think must have been a new firm—called De Havillands. It was a new urban engineering firm that was starting to make, around about the time of the beginning of the 1st World War, aircraft for the new Royal Flying Corps, in Britain. Grandpa as a designer was very excited to help in this process, and as someone who had extraordinary knowledge, and skills in dealing with laminated woods and other innovative ways of developing wood products, he designed and helped make aircraft propellers for De Havillands for the Royal Flying Corps.

This he seemed to do during the 1st World War, by which time at least two of his sons became of military age and were, unlike the situation in Czarist Russia, happy and proud to go off and serve King and country. Morris, the eldest son, volunteered for the K.O.Y.L.I.'s—the King's own Yorkshire Light Infantry, and went off to the Western Front in France, where later he was to make a name for himself as a signaller—reconnecting damaged and destroyed signalling connections at the front. Belatedly, he was to be recognised for his work by being made a "Chevalier de la Legion d'honneur" by the French Government. His brother Jack was even more adventurous, and after a term in the British Army, went off to Canada to join the Canadian army. He went with the Canadian army to the Western Front in France, where he was gassed, and had big problems recuperating from that attack. Eventually, he went back to do extraordinary things in North America. However, we'll hear more about him in 'Tales of the Wild Ones' later in this book.

After the First World War, there was no longer a future for designers of propellers of wooden aircraft, as the developments in the 1st World War led on to the creation of metal propellers, and so it seems Grandpa became unemployed in Leeds, and somehow or other, again for reasons which I do not know, and have never been able to understand, he moved to Cardiff in South Wales, and there he settled down.

Unable to find work as a designer, he was trying hard to find a job, in what was a growing economic depression. Thus in the Great Depression we find that Grandpa Michael had opened and developed, surprisingly, a large fish and chip shop in Central Cardiff!! This became one of the features of the city, and one of the most popular venues for the crowds on their way to and from the Cardiff City football matches, at Ninian Park, to call in at his place, which had the best fish and chips in Cardiff! It seems that at some stage Michael's son—Morris, became the President of the South Wales Fish Fryers Association, organising their annual charabanc outings to the Brecon Beacons, or to the Coast!

However, to continue the story, which becomes very affected by the initiatives of Morris—about whom we will hear in the next chapter. The family—by stages, moved to New Zealand, (!!) It was there—in New Zealand, that all of the Travis family, Grandpa—with three of his four sons, were to settle down in the capital city of Wellington, to a new and different life. This became a rich family-life, but one that was shortly to be affected by the surprise coming of war, the 2nd World War, which very much affected New Zealand. More news about this critical time, and the furniture factory venture, will be told in dad's story, which comes next in the book.

That story of New Zealand in war, and at war, is a fascinating one in itself, and it's a separate chapter, which will come later. What is more important to explain at this point, is that Grandpa Michael who had retired, was enjoying life in this interesting 100 years' young city. Suddenly one day—during the war, he received a very official letter, which had an unusual mark on the envelope outside, indicating that it was from the Governor-General's office, and he is the senior representative of the Queen in New Zealand! Grandpa opened the letter, and we all read this extraordinary communication. It stated that from records, the New Zealand branch of De Havillands had discovered that Grandpa had been employed by them in the 1st World War in Leeds, on propeller design work. There was now—in the middle of this new War, a secret project to go ahead on the development in Australia and New Zealand of a special new aircraft, (namely to be the prototype of the 'Australasian Mosquito'), which was to be all-wooden, including wooden propellers! There were no longer designers available who could design and make wooden propellers. Yet it was known that Grandpa—who had these skills—was alive, and was in New Zealand, so they would welcome it if he would come out of retirement, and help the War-effort. This would be by training-up young men in New Zealand, to design, and to make wooden propellers for the Mosquito project.

To cut a long story short, Grandpa came out of retirement, and spent what must have been a year or two in this training and supervisory task at De Havillands Aircraft Factory, at Rongotai, in Wellington. Thus grandpa aided the Australasian version of the Mosquito Aircraft, which was built, and was used in the Pacific War, just as the U.K. version of the plane—was used in the European War.

Sadly, Grandpa was never recognised for this important work that he did in two World Wars helping first of all the home country, and secondly the two dominions "Down Under". Perhaps this was because he by origin was seen as a 'foreigner', for though naturalised, he was not British-born, but he was passionately patriotic, and was proud to have served his country in two World Wars.

CHAPTER TWO

Morris—The Perfect English Country-man

Thinking about my dad, Morris, it is hard for me to realise that he was the first child of immigrants born in a village north of London, as everything about him made him the archetypal "perfect English country-man, or country gentleman". To have seen him dressed characteristically in his tweeds, and smoking his pipe, walking in the countryside, lighting-up his pipe, visiting church graveyards and looking at the headstones, and contemplating the lives of families who had lived in this Worcestershire village, or that, it is hard for me to think that dad was not someone who had come from a long line of English country folk!

His early life in Edmonton village, as it then was, must have been a fairly rough and complex one, as his family had limited means. I'm not sure when and how he started his schooling, but as the son of parents—both of whom were hard-working, it's clear that from a very early age he was the one who always guided, and kept an eye on what became his three younger brothers. With only the church graveyard to play in, and other local boys to fight with, because these were strangers in the village, it must have been a difficult start to life here, in England.

My father, died in 1999, and had been born in 1898, so he was 101 when he died, but I never heard him say anything about an early life in California, so I'm still not clear whether he and his brothers were taken to live in California or not. Perhaps they were left with relatives, because by the early 1900s—some other members of my Grandpa's Polish family had also come to live in the London and Leeds areas.

Dad's early life, must have spanned a period in Edmonton and certainly also in Leeds. I'm not sure exactly which year it was that they settled in Leeds, but there they lived in very modest circumstances, in an area of Leeds which seems to have been inhabited by recent immigrants. There he developed—much to my intrigue, a gentle Yorkshire accent, which he retained for the rest of his life.

He looked older than his age, so that by the time that Morris was about 15 he was already being given white feathers in Leeds. The young women thought he was of military age, which he was not, and they considered therefore that he should be volunteering for the army, which he was actually too young to join!! As his father was already doing war-work, and his mother was ill, with her heart problems, he may have found it difficult to look after the three younger brothers.

Morris seems to have had to look after his siblings in those early days, and I'm not sure at what stage he started to go out to work. Surprisingly, his father apprenticed him to a tailor, and he was sent for several months to learn tailoring with my Grandpa's brother-in-law, who by then had a tailoring shop, or what I would call "a sweat shop" in the East End of London. There—at one stage, Morris was trained as a tailor, but I do not know if this was before, or after his period of military service.

Perhaps at this point one needs to say something about dad's character. He was essentially an Edwardian, a very moral man of great integrity, who was of medium height, with 'Ronald Colman type good looks', and complete with the subtle moustache. Dressing well and appropriately was important to him—whether with his 1920's straw boater or wearing a suede zipper for a charabanc outing, his dark felt trilbies in the 30's, or choosing the right casual wear for a fishing trip in the 1940's. He took the Ten Commandments very seriously, and was motivated above all by the one which stated that "you must honour your father and your mother . . . .". His devotion to his parents, at times damaged not only his own interests, but also those of his wife and children. Had he been born in a later generation, he had the quality of mind that would have enabled him to go to University, where he would have made a very good electrical engineering student.

What is clear is that during his time in the King's Own Yorkshire Light Infantry, when he was sent to France, and did valued work as a signaller on the Western Front, that in the reading material which he had with him and devoured, were books about Captain Cook and New Zealand. He became obsessed with the idea that that new country, which was discovered by Captain Cook, and later settled by English Settlers,& called New Zealand, was really "the promised land" for him, and it was the place where he dearly wanted to go, and to live after the 1st World War.

Morris with his late 1930's "Ronald Colman good looks".

Whilst this overriding aim was there in the background, dad in daily life always enjoyed meeting people. He could never go on a tram, a train, or bus, without getting into conversation confidently with strangers, and by chatting to folks, find out their life-stories!

In the early 1920s in Cardiff, living with his father, & his sick mother, he was persuaded, again surprisingly, into developing a large fish and chip shop, in the Riverside district of Cardiff. There he, his father, and later—his wife, and assistants, developed this thriving and popular business. This was the livelihood that enabled the four boys to reach maturity, and then later—one by one—shake their wings, like birds in the nest, and fly far away, as young birds do.

Morris however, never forgot his dream and wish about going to New Zealand, and so in 1922 he sent his younger brother Joss (as Joshua was known), to a new life in the new country. There he settled down, and initially found a job travelling as a commercial traveller across North Island, New Zealand. He went to the remote King Country, and got to know villages, farm-stations (as they are called), and towns right across the extensive North Island of the country, and was even able to find a potential N.Z.-born wife, called Lily, in Wellington City!

The 1920's were a difficult and demanding decade for Morris. He constantly had to defer his planned migration to New Zealand, because of meeting the needs of others. His brother Jack disappeared to North America, and much time was taken searching for him. The Depression forced much effort to go into the family business, but as his mother was dying of heart failure, he was the one who had both to nurse her, and also to guide his brothers.

He got married in 1925 to Esther Seligman, his first son (Conrad) was born a year later—in 1926, and then his mother died in that same year. At the start of the 1930's, economic circumstances were difficult for all, a second son was born in 1932 (namely myself), and the reactions to all the cumulative pressures upon dad, led to him having a collapse in 1933, with nervous exhaustion. This led to his going off to Boscombe (near Bournemouth) for a period of rest and recuperation.

A further complication was that in 1932, immediately after having given birth to me, my mother was required to make the wedding for Uncle Joss. He had returned on a visit, with his new potential bride from New Zealand, to get married in Cardiff, before returning to N.Z.! By 1936 Uncle Harry, who had already married his wife Bella, and had a young daughter Audrey, set off to settle in New Zealand. This left only my Grandpa, my parents, my brother and myself behind in Cardiff.

Though our emigration had also been planned for 1936 or '37, it seems that unfortunately young Tony prevented this. He seemed to get every conceivable schoolchild illness, from Measles, and Whooping Cough to Mumps, thus delaying our emigration until 1939. It was in that year that at last we set sail for New Zealand, leaving London's Port of Tilbury in the S.S. Orford, an Orient Line Liner, on its four week long sea trip to Australia. There we then boarded a second ship, the S.S.Wanganella, sailing on for a further 4 day sea journey to New Zealand. The story of that incredible travel in the year 1939, will be told in another chapter in this book.

1939 to 1940 was a momentous piece of timing for the family to come together in Wellington in New Zealand. Already war shadows were looming, and of course with the start of the European War in 1939, and problems in the Pacific Ocean sphere affecting Australia and New Zealand in 39-40, world events were to impinge upon the family and on their new lives in New Zealand. We temporarily moved into a house in Ghuznee Street in central Wellington in 1939, staying there for a short time before we moved to a flat in the old suburb of Newtown in the same year. We then found ourselves living next to the Dexton home.

This was an extraordinary neighbour to have, because we were living next to a home, where there were perhaps 60 to 80 teenagers, who had been brought from Poland to New Zealand, by a generous New Zealand family, to save them from the impacts of impending war. These were Jewish boys and girls, all with wonderful biblical names like Reuben and Ruth, who also found themselves in a new country. They were the older playmates that I found next door for my brother, myself, as well as for my lovely cousin Audrey, who lived nearby.

By 1940 we moved on to a nicer suburb namely Kilbirnie, where I went to my second NZ primary school—Lyall Bay School. Then we finally moved to our last, and what we thought was going to be our permanent home—in Miramar, in 1943. Thus it was that in Wellington all the Travis family, as it then became, were re-united. The two brothers in New Zealand had already changed their name to 'Travis,' which was more acceptable there than 'Tavrogis'. We too were to have our surname changed by deed-poll, so that we all became Travises, in N.Z.

The big project in 1940 was the furniture factory project. This was a purpose built-factory, which was realised, by the coming together in business of Grandpa, and three of his sons, to create in the Kilbirnie district of Wellington, a factory making new furniture for the New Zealand market. The problem was obviously one of timing, and by the time the factory was completed and operational, war conditions were prevailing in New Zealand. Thus, within a short time, the factory had to close down, as one uncle went into the Forces, my father was 'man-powered', and had to go into essential war-work, and thus the whole furniture factory venture was a sad disaster.

"Man-powering" meant that dad was taken out of his civilian occupation, and was obliged to join the Shell Oil Company in Miramar. There he spent many months—if not years, moving oil drums and doing other heavy war work. This led to him suffering injuries when one or two people with whom he was working, let go of the heavy oil drums, with him then taking the full weight, so damaging his back and one of his legs. Despite this injury, he had no compensation, but was released at that stage from war work. Later he first opened a temporary shop in Kilbirnie, but that soon gave way to his opening a hardware and garden plant shop in Hataitai.

Here he found fulfilment in doing something which was an enormous source of pleasure to him, helping and advising people on their odd jobs, hardware needs, and do-it-yourself activities in their homes. In addition he was of course buying and selling garden plants, which was a great source of delight to him as a keen gardener, and as someone who enjoyed going out to the plant-nurseries in the Hutt Valley. In this difficult time of transition, one of the few very good and happy memories was of the holiday that my father, mother, and myself had in the Marlborough Sounds. To go there, we travelled by the old ferry steamer the S.S. Tamahine, which took three or four hours to cross the Cook Strait to South Island, and there we stayed in the Hotel Terminus in the little resort town of Picton.

Particular memories are of a day's fishing trip on which dad and I went. There it was the habit for the men folk of two or three families to hire jointly a sea motor cruiser and its crew for a day's fishing for Blue Cod, in the Sounds. The men took their sons with them, and thus we all enjoyed a day in the sun, deep sea fishing. All went well, until—through a bad line cast, on the part of one of the other fishermen, a fishing hook went right through dad's hand. Consequently, he had to sit there smoking his pipe and turning different colours, as they sawed off the barbs of the hook—so as to be able to pull out this out from his hand!

However, in the evening, in a happier vein, the boat pulled into a remote cove with a sandy beach that was backed by native tree-ferns, and wild bush. There, the freshly caught fish were placed in holes dug in the sand, and cooked Maori-style, with ferns over the fish, and hot stones beneath them. Whilst we all lay back on the sands, someone started strumming a guitar, and others provided cans of Waitemata beer to drink, whilst we waited for the fish to cook. The moon came out by the time we were eating the succulent fish, and listening to the gentle music. It was, for a special moment—an idyllic evening, in a time of war.

The pattern of war, defence, and family being away in the armed forces, was rarely broken up by special family events, such as big musical evenings. That is when Uncle Harry would play on his ukulele, my cousin Audrey would play the piano, mum, dad and I would sing, and there would be a great sense of fun. There were a few rare times, when we could all get together for a family Passover or Pesach event. Then my aunts would be busy baking, my father and uncles (when on leave), would argue about all sorts of exciting ideas, in what was basically the biblical story of Exodus, or a festival devoted to the precious idea of freedom.

The forties for me, despite the war, was a wonderful time of having all of the Travis family together in Wellington in New Zealand between their absences due to war service. Though a time of war, one could still have fun doing those things that make N.Z. a child's paradise. One could go tobogganing down over the pine needles which carpet the pine forest, in the high hills that forms the 'Town Belt' of Wellington, or go to the zoo in Newtown. Some treats—like sea canoeing in the vast waters of Wellington Harbour, were best left to safer enjoyment—after the War.

What was growingly difficult, however, for my mother, was that she became increasingly unhappy, especially after her friend—my Aunt Bella, died at a very young age due to cancer, and my mother felt increasingly isolated. Dad had all of his immediate family nearby in New Zealand, but she felt that she had no-one there, her family were far away—in the 'Old Country', ie The British Isles.

Thus in the post-war period a growing friction was present in the family, between dad who was increasingly happy in New Zealand,

and my mother. She felt isolated from her parental family, did not like the occasional New Zealand earthquakes which we had, and wanted very much to go back on a visit to see her mother and brother in England. Her brother had now been demobbed from the UK army, after serving overseas. Thus it was that plans emerged for a trip that—at first, she was going to make alone, to Britain after the war. There were however, extreme problems of shipping shortage in that post-war period, and in 1945 my mother would have liked to have gone back immediately on a holiday. However, it was not until 1946 that the prospect of such a holiday became more realistic, in terms of shipping availability.

However, it was found that though she could get a shipping-passage to Britain, which was in those days—a five week journey by sea, she could get no guarantee of return shipping for two years. This proposition led to a great family crisis, as my father was not prepared to have his wife away from him for two years! So, after much discussion and argument, it was proposed that the whole family would go on an extended holiday visit to Britain, on which I was to be taken, and on which my Grandpa wanted to join, as well.

After a long sea-journey back to the U.K., of five weeks plus via the Panama Canal, we went back to Cardiff. We did not go to Bournemouth—where dad by nature would have preferred to have gone. Going back to Cardiff was a big mistake, because there dad still owned a property, which had been rented out to tenants, when we were in NZ,. Thus started his battle under the Rent Restrictions Act, to try and get back occupancy of that building. During this time we lived in a hotel, and that stay, which initially was planned for a few weeks, came to last over a year, and was financially disastrous. This led eventually to dad's decision to phone his brother, my Uncle Harry, in New Zealand, to sell our house there, and send over our furniture and belongings from New Zealand to Wales.

He eventually got re-possession of that property, opened an adjacent shop, and for years struggled with that shop. Later he started a new shop which he opened, selling quality fruits and vegetables in the Castle Arcade, in the centre of Cardiff. Thus what had been a family holiday became our re-migration to the Old Country. It was here, after a period of three months or so, that it was decided that I should continue my schooling. Arrangements were made for me to join Cardiff High School, which was a very good boys' grammar school in the city of Cardiff. However, I was to have a long period of adjustment to life in a different country. In those days—with my strong New Zealand accent, I was the subject of ridicule and humour in the new school which I attended. I did eventually settle in well, despite the different education system, and adjusted to the new life here, in what was a rather grey, and sad post-war Britain, still feeling all the severe after-effects of the Second World War.

This was also a difficult period for my parents, as things went very badly with the new shop. Dad had to face bankruptcy, he longingly looked back to life in New Zealand, and my mother constantly teased him about "the monument he was building to his past life there"—so it was not an easy time in the family, then.

However, from my personal point of view, though there were many problems for the family at this time, I was the one who was to have the long term advantages of our coming back to the Old Country. This was because it is here that I had an excellent continuing grammar school education, and later university education. Thus I had very long term gains that I may or may not have had, if our life had continued as it was in the past, in New Zealand.

By 1951, I was coming to the end of my schooling in the U.K., and though the offer had been there of a place to study history in Cambridge University, I chose to go to Manchester University, where a five year honours degree in this new subject of Town and Country Planning, was newly available. This was a subject which I had become obsessed about, during my years at grammar school in Cardiff, where in hours spent visiting the Cardiff Central Library, I had read all their books on Town Planning, and became familiar with the writings of Geddes, Mumford, and Abercrombie.

When I went off to University in 1951, it was just a few months after my Grandpa had died, so, with my brother also away from home, mum and dad became 'Derby and Joan' in what became their retirement. This was first in Penarth, and later in a council-flat out on the Llanrumney Estate, to the east of Cardiff. There dad became active once again, as president of a local residents association, and was busy making local friends. Sadly my mother's health was deteriorating, and it was from here that she went into hospital, and died in the year 1972. Dad lived on in his flat until he was 96, and then had to be persuaded—because of his failing eyesight, and other problems—to go and become a resident in a nearby old age home. There he stayed until his death at the age of 101, in the year 1999. At his hundredth birthday, he had been in great form, for the last time.

Looking back upon dad's life, it's best to remember him when he was at his happiest, such as when I went with him up to Belmont, in the Hutt Valley to the North of Wellington. There he would visit the garden-nurseries run by a friend of his, and choose the boxes of plants and small trees, which he would take back by train to Wellington for selling in his shop in Hataitai. On these days he was very relaxed, as he was also in his free time at home—repairing, doing electrics, gardening, and being an odd-jobber, that fitted very much into the New Zealand mould. Everyone in N.Z. "has a go at everything", and provided things work more or less, every man says 'Well, she'll do!'

Walking with dad through the native bush in the green hills of the Marlborough Sounds, seeing him happy and relaxed smoking his pipe, and reminiscing about life, one recognised a truly fulfilled man who had found the life he wanted, in the country that he loved.

Nothing perhaps damaged him more than having to move away from that idyllic land, to a sad old country, which was grey and tired, and in which he saw the latter days of his life. Here in Britain, in Cardiff he died in the year 1999. Had he lived one more year he would have experienced life in three centuries, as he was born in the 19th Century, lived throughout the 20th Century, s and almost made it into the 21st.

Dad was a fine, confident, and noble human being. He certainly was not a businessman, and some people even viewed him as an economic failure. However, he was an enormous success—as a human being! Though he died over twelve years ago, he is someone whom I think of, and still miss, daily.

CHAPTER THREE

New Zealand At War

Here in the U.K. everyone is used to what historians call a "Euro-centric view" of World War Two, which is inevitable. There was a very different view of the war from New Zealand. Whilst the European War was very much focussed upon the actions of Nazi Germany and Fascist Italy, the Asia-Pacific War was the one against Imperial Japan. In this context, it's important to remember that there were critical sea-routes, which kept the Empire alive. They were both for the movement of migrants from the Old Country to new countries—such as the Dominions of Canada, Australia and New Zealand, but also as vital links for trade, for the import of raw materials and natural products from the Commonwealth, and the export there of manufactured goods from the U.K.

Thus New Zealand had been tied to Britain, relying on access via the Suez & Panama Canal routes. The safety of these sea routes from New Zealand via Australia was vital, and of course for the import of manufactured goods from Britain, as well as receiving flows of migrants. Critically for the New Zealand economy, the sea-routes were for the sending of New Zealand's agricultural products to the home market, here in the UK. Thus the continuing production of lamb, mutton, beef, butter, cheese, & apples, relied on their long journey by refrigerated vessels to the UK, for sale. War put at risk this vital trade, so that war itself meant that the New Zealand economy fundamentally had to face the risk of not being able to export to Britain, nor being able to import the manufactured goods from the Old Country. The involvement and commitment to Britain of people "Down Under," led to the early sending of airmen, and later troops, to help in the fight against Nazi Europe, as well as in the war against Imperial Japan.

From 1939 to '40 onwards the New Zealand economy was having to adjust radically to a changed situation. It had to become much more self-reliant, because even the import of products from the United States was risky, due to the attacks upon shipping in the Pacific by the Japanese warships and submarines. In fact shipping was the lifeline of New Zealand, whether in terms of the sea-routes, passenger-liners, and cargo ships, going to and from Britain, via the two Canals, or via the Tasman shipping, which connected New Zealand and Australia, and—for that matter—the internal shipping which connected the two islands of New Zealand. Two key internal shipping routes were those from Wellington to Picton, which was the main link to South Island, and secondly the longer sea route from Wellington to Port Lyttleton, which is the port for Christchurch, the largest city on the South Island.

My view of the Second World War is that of a youngster, who experienced the 1939 to 1945 war as a boy growing from 7 to 13 years old, living in the capital of New Zealand, Wellington. Initially it seemed an unreal war, because what was happening in Europe was very distant, and the war in Asia and the Pacific was initially concentrated on China, and then upon Pacific islands, starting with Formosa, and going on to the Philippines, and to the Malay Peninsula.

Furthermore, 1940 was an important year in another sense for New Zealand, because it was celebrating its 100 years since the

Treaty of Waitangi, and the resultant free settlement of white migrants (or Pakehas) in Maori, New Zealand. For 1940, the country had been preparing and had built a great centennial exhibition, which occupied a large site in the eastern suburbs of Wellington, and this great exhibition opened in 1940. It was assumed, was going to attract visitors not only from New Zealand and Australia, but also from Europe and from the United States! As the exhibition took place in Rongotai—the next district to Kilbirnie, where we then lived—it was somewhere I got to know well, with its pavilions, exhibits, its water features, its fun fairs and all. Sadly, most of the expected visitors never came, and the exhibition closed prematurely—under the impacts of war time conditions. The early disappearance of many of New Zealand's young men, to fight overseas was notable. They went as pilots in the RAF, or as troops going to join the 8th Army in the Middle East or Expeditionary Forces going to Hong Kong, Singapore, and elsewhere to reinforce key imperial strategic points, early in the Second World War.

Soon you realised that many people had gone away. The sons of neighbouring families had left—as airmen off to fight in the Battle of Britain, relations of friends at school, had sailed off to defend, what was called the 'Singapore fortress', and

View of Wellignton, New Zealand, in the 1940's.

others went to Hong Kong. The absence of young men in New Zealand was notable, for with universal call-up there, they all the disappeared overseas, and the young women went into essential services. Older men, like my father—were "man-powered" (ie compulsorily directed) to do essential war work in N.Z.

I've already mentioned how, early-on, living in the flat next to the large Dexton Home, we'd got to know these Polish teenagers. Thus we were aware of distant societies, and problems, a long way away from New Zealand, but which had some effects there. Also, in 1939, my Grandpa had had a letter from his cousins in Poland, to whom he had written—trying to encourage to emigrate to New Zealand, but who had written back saying that even if war came, they felt they would be unaffected in Poland! All but one of them, were to die in the Holocaust.

I've already told the story, in the last chapter, of how the timing of building the family's furniture factory was disastrously impacted upon by the coming of war. Of course, the family too was splitting-up, through one uncle going into the army, my brother prematurely disappearing to try and get into the armed forces, dad going into war-work, and a little later Grandpa getting called-up for his special war-time tasks. Gradually, through listening to the news daily on the radio, and seeing all sorts of changes that were taking place, war impacted more and more upon daily-life. Whilst basic foods were in generous supply in New Zealand, because we were not able to export all our food surpluses to Britain, many things were short, all sorts of food stuffs and products that normally came from Britain and the United States could not be imported, because of shipping crises.

The Japanese threat became ever greater, so that by the time of the Battle of the Pearl Sea, one feared that New Zealand would soon be invaded. It had very little in the way of defences, as its naval vessels had been sent to fight with the Royal Navy, its Air force was minimal, it's young men were overseas, and it was having to prepare schoolboys and old men to deal with the expected invasion of New Zealand.

The treacherous Japanese attack upon Pearl Harbour, brought the U.S.A. into the Pacific War. It was then that the Americans started to come, in large numbers: U.S. Marines and G.I.s arriving by troop-ship, ready for the Pacific War. They were stationed in large numbers, in bases in and around Wellington, prior to their despatch to key island battles in the Pacific, from Guadalcanal onwards. Because of the jokingly referred to 'American Occupation', A.F.N. or the American Forces Network for the South Pacific, became located in Wellington. Thus it was possible occasionally to go with my mother to the live recording of radio concerts, by great American bands—like Artie Shaw's, which visited New Zealand to entertain the troops, and to broadcast to them—throughout the South Pacific.

At school we were even given training for survival in the Bush. It was expected that when the Japanese occupation took place, we would need to hide & survive in the Bush, and to harass the Japanese occupiers, as a resistance force. Thus as youngsters we were taught how to use .303 rifles, and how to dig slit-trenches for the expected air raids. The seriousness of the war was coming home to everyone, when the Japanese started their aerial bombing of Port Darwin, in Northern Australia, and Japanese submarines sank shipping in Sydney Harbour. Japanese submarines were also attacking shipping around the coasts of New Zealand, including attempted sinking of the inter-island steamers.

New Zealand entertainers had gone overseas to help entertain both New Zealand and also American troops abroad. I found that by the time that I was eleven, I was helping others of my age group to form concert-parties, to entertain American troops in Wellington. I recall going to the St. George Hotel in the city centre of Wellington, where I did both impressions of the popular crooner—Bing Crosby's songs, and also some of Carmen Miranda's, as well! The war became increasingly long and complex: news came through of more and more human losses due to the war, the neighbour's sons had died at Monte Casino in Italy, and a woman we met on holiday, heard that her husband had been shot down, whilst fighting with the RNZAF overseas. Belatedly, after the atomic bombing of Nagasaki and Hiroshima, the Pacific War eventually came to an end, and the prospect of peace came, with many question-marks for the Travis family.

A curious war-time recollection, in view of the injustices and racism that was being fought in the Second World War, relates to two holidays I had as a youngster, staying up-country in a farm near Dannevirke. The Dannevirke area, near Napier, was perhaps three or four hours rail journey from Wellington, and had been settled early in the 20th Century by Danish farmers. They had brought with them all of their prejudices from rural Denmark. Thus, when I arrived to stay on a farm at Umutaoroa, I was greeted suspiciously by the children and friends of the family with which I was staying, and it was not until the first full day there, that I was taken out into a field and surrounded by a group of fairly hostile looking youngsters, who turned and asked me if I was a Catholic! I explained that no, I was not a Catholic, but neither was I a Protestant, as I happened to be Jewish. They replied 'oh that's okay, but because of the way we feel about Catholics in this Protestant community, had you said you were a Catholic, we'd have probably hanged you'.

This memory has long stayed with me as I've always hated all forms of prejudice, be it anti-Catholic, anti-Protestant, anti-Jewish, or anti-Black, and the transfer of this old world prejudice to a free new country, like New Zealand, shocked me very deeply. Such prejudice was to be encountered again, many years later in my life, when—as a consultant I did work in Northern Ireland. There—in official circles I found appalling anti-Catholic prejudice, which led to my resignation from contract work in Northern Ireland. The reason was that I was not prepared to tolerate appalling prejudices on the part of a Board Chairman, and of some of the officials, with whom I had to work.

1945 was a transitional year—part war, and part-peace. I was happily settled in my new life in second year at a very special secondary school—Rongotai College, which was an easy tram-ride for me on the No.2 tram, from our home in Miramar! More will be heard of Rongotai, in the chapter on "The Scottish Diaspora".

We were now three teenage Travis grand-children : my brother Con, my cousin Audrey, and myself, plus cousin Valerie-who was younger than us. This happy 'gang' of young Travii, were very much in evidence at our big June event in Wellington—my 13th birthday, and Barmitzvah! A very welcome post-war addition to the Travis family, was Valerie's new baby brother—Barrie, my first male cousin! Sadly, due to our departure from New Zealand in 1946, I did not have the pleasure of getting to know Barrie, until many years later, when we were both adult.

Though 1946 was the first year of peace, it proved to be a time of great pending change for the family. However, three water–related trips were highlights of our latter period as NZ residents. The first was a holiday journey on the S.S. Rangatira to Port Lyttleton, with a stay in the lovely city of Christchurch, secondly day-trips on the Cobar ferry, across Wellington Harbour to the resort of Days Bay, and third and best of all—a special canoe trip! The canoe trip with my Hataitai friend Lindsay Linney, from Rongotai College, set out from the Patent Slip-on Evans Bay, and took us out into the vastness of Wellington Harbour. It was a day I was to long remember. All too soon, though, talk was of a much longer family sea journey—to the U.K.! New Zealand changed a great deal as a result of the Second World War. It changed politically from having for 30 or 40 years been a Labour country, to voting-in later—a National Government, (ie a Conservative Government), and removing all its subsidies to agriculture, so that market-forces were fundamentally to change New Zealand. It lost some forms of its extensive agriculture, and developed new intensive vitri-culture. Thus the country, in the post-war world, became a great wine producer, developing new markets and new successes. Also, attitudes became changed. New Zealand and New Zealanders became more and more oriented to the outside world, with younger Kiwis starting to go on six week trips to Europe and to the Americas, as everyone wanted to know more about the outside world. By the 1960's, air flights connecting New Zealand, Australia, and Britain, were gradually to become the norm, replacing the long and time-demanding sea-journeys, and making the world that much smaller. Remote New Zealand thus became very much involved in the new and smaller globe.

The eight years of living in New Zealand, were for me the critical formative years of my life. Their impact was to make me a kiwi, in terms of spirit, knowledge, and attitudes. However, because dad had continued to own property in the U.K., when we were in NZ, British passports were retained, both for him and his family, so we failed to get NZ passports. It is a sadness for me that I remained a "Pom" or a "Brit", and did not formally become a New Zealander.

CHAPTER FOUR

The Sad Tale of Essie

The next story which I want to tell, is a tale about a young woman—who was made a casualty by a difficult parental marriage, largely caused by the hard character of a father. It makes one wonder about the issue of 'nature' versus 'nurture'. In other words, how far are we shaped by our genetic or inherited characteristics, and how far are we affected by our family upbringing, or environment? The girl at the heart of this story was named Esther, who was known as 'Essie', and she was my mother.

Esther was born in 1904 in Swansea, the second child born to two immigrant parents. The father Hyman Zeligman had been born in 1879 in Lodz, in Czarist Poland. Her mother was Rebecca Jackson,(originally Zarchin). She was known as Milly, and was born in 1881 in White Russia. Milly's parents had been timber merchants in a remote, rural, forested-area, where their family also had a 'half-way house', which was a type of rural hotel.

Essie's father's character is a critical factor in this story. He was a strictly religious man, an orthodox Jew who daily went to pray at a local Beth Hamedresh (or prayer-house). He was stern in character and had two work roles. They were those of a credit-draper on the one hand, and as a Zionist organiser on the other. Esther described him as a cruel man, whilst her step-brother David, recently described him to me as being "stern and ultra religious". Esther's father was to be married twice. In this first marriage his wife gave birth to four children, a son—Max, then a daughter Esther, and two more sons-Ruben & Mossie. Hyman was to marry again later on, after his divorce, and father three more sons—in his second marriage. Esther's mother too, after the divorce from her first husband, was also to marry a second time. Married life for Essie's parents started in Swansea, a Welsh industrial city 50 miles or so to the west of the capital. The Zeligman family later moved to Cardiff itself, where the family established itself in the Riverside district.

Perhaps at this point, it would be helpful to say something about the character of Esther herself. By appearance from her childhood onwards, she was slim, attractive, and a person who liked to dress well, but simply, and appropriately. She had long hair in her youth, and a rather gentle voice. She showed a great love of music from early in her life, largely focussing upon opera, and musical comedy. Her life-time knowledge of many operatic arias and popular songs, plus her good singing voice, enabled her to sing attractively, wherever she was, and whatever she was doing. Later she was to sing in choirs. Because of her love of music and the theatre, she was to get enormous enjoyment from West End theatre musicals, when that became possible later in life. She was a very free spirit, adaptable, and resilient. Thus she was the one who was first to react against her father's authoritarianism. She came from a family on her maternal side, the Jacksons, who were rather gentler, less religious, warmer, and friendlier then the Zeligmans. Her father seemed to lack a sense of humour, whereas Esther—from an early stage in life, gave evidence of a warm and lively sense of humour. Thus, in many ways, Esther was extremely different to her dad, and the seeds of conflict were inherent.

I know that at an early age, after completing primary school, she left home, running away so as to be with her aunt and uncle in Birmingham, before moving on to London. I am still not clear exactly what age she was, but it seems to have been somewhere between the

A study of Essie as a young woman, in the early 1920's.

age of 11 and 14. She had the guts to take the rash action of leaving the repressive family home, and going to stay with her warm and very compatible Uncle Sam and Auntie Rae Jackson. It is perhaps evidential of the sort of pressures at home in the Zeligmans, that two of Esther's brothers left home as soon as they could do so. Her elder brother Max, who had trained at Cardiff Technical College in his teens to become a lawyer, left home by the age of 20, to go to Mandatory British Palestine in 1922. A picture of life in Mandatory Palestine can be found in the books by Holliday, Samuel and Segev. Max's brother

Rueben left home a year or two later, to go to settle in Australia! Only one son was to remain in the family home, and that was the youngest son—Moss. Consequently, he was squashed down by the process of living with his repressive father. Thus he became a quiet and withdrawn character, whose only passion in life was stamp collecting.

It is hard now to piece together the whole pattern of Essie's period away from her family in Cardiff. Whilst I know that she did for a period go to stay with the Jackson uncle and aunt in Birmingham, I don't know exactly when she moved on to London. I still do not know whether she lived with the other Jackson uncle—namely Bob, in London, or whether she lived independently there, What I do know is that she went to work as a shop assistant in the West End of London, and for several years worked on sales—in a fashion shop, in Central London. She enjoyed being with a team of young, compatible, work-mates, and occasionally going out to West End theatre shows. Such evenings must have been a source of great delight to her, with her strong musical interests.

By the 1920's she had returned to Cardiff, but I'm still not clear as to whether then she was living there with her mother, or with whom?, However, by 1925—or early 1926, she had married my father, Morris, and moved into the large corner house at 80 Tudor Road together with her husband, her father-in-law. Her father was living two doors away, in no.84 Tudor Road! By the end of 1926, the first child (Conrad), had been born to the young couple—Esther and Morris, who were now working very hard, helping in the new fish and chip shop. A male colleague was doing some of the heavy manual work in the shop, and soon a young girl from the Valleys, was brought to help look after the baby boy.

Both of my parents were working full-time in the business. Conrad, the first son born late in 1926, was a hearty extrovert, who fitted well into this fairly free and independent existence. Everything was possible for a young lad, with both his parents and his grandfather busy working. From an early age the first-born child had the freedom to take many initiatives. It was not until the second child was born in 1932, namely my own arrival, that my mother had apparently certain health-problems in the delivery. She had recurrent health-problems after I was born. In consequence, this slim young woman who had been an attractive 'flapper', suddenly put on excessive weight, and changed considerably in appearance.

The 1930's were a time of economic depression, so with work pressures, two children, as well as a business to look after, this was a demanding time for both of my parents. As a result, they did not know exactly if and when—they would be moving to settle in New Zealand!

I've already indicated earlier in the book, that it was not until 1939, that the move to New Zealand did take place! It was later—after complex local moves occurred in Wellington, that the family and my mother seemed to settle down well. That was first in Kilbirnie, and later in our home in Miramar. However, as indicated earlier in the book, the death of her sister-in-law, Auntie Bella, who was a warm, lively, and most compatible person, was an enormous blow to Essie. Her other sister-in-law, Lily, Uncle Joss's wife, was a very different character to the late Bella. She was a rather hard, competitive, and self-centred woman, who showed little sympathy, let alone give any real support to my mother. Thus Essie felt, as I've already indicated before, increasingly isolated. Thus she started to imagine that things would be much better if, somehow, she could see again her family in England.

Perhaps this was something of an unreal dream though, as the family in England did not represent very much in the way of solidarity. Perhaps, it was only the case, in terms of her mother's compatible Jackson relatives. However, in 1946, when we did eventually return on this trip to Britain, it was somewhat disillusioning for my mother to link up again with people she considered her own family. Her mother had remarried, and when we went to visit that couple in their house in Finsbury Park in North London, I recall that my mother was given a rather cool reception, which was deeply upsetting for her. She saw her brother Mossie again, but that link was nowhere near as strong, as she thought. When we did see her Jackson uncles—ie. Uncle Sam and Uncle Bob, they were as warm and as welcoming as one could have hoped them to be.

Her brother Max, who had been long settled in Palestine, was busy with his professional life as a successful international lawyer, who had offices by the 1940s in Tel Aviv, Montreal, Johannesburg, and London. He could barely find time to contact, let alone see his one sister. When I first saw them together in the postwar period, he struck me as disinterested. He was very focussed upon his own business affairs, and had his own direct family, comprising his Canadian wife, and two grown-up, daughters. Thus the much wished—for return to the Old Country by mum, proved to be a very mixed blessing! She liked to be back in Cardiff, which she still thought of as home, but even more—she loved to go up to London, which with its great West End theatre life and musical life, seemed the real Mecca!. So perhaps, though her latter days were spent in Cardiff, she was never truly fulfilled—as a person. She would come to life when socialising, cooking, and singing happily, but much of the time she was an insecure person. When references to marriage cropped up in conversations, she always used the phrase 'not till death do us part, but till divorce do us part'. The idea of divorce and separation seemed in-grained in her very being, because of those experiences in both her father's and mother's lives.

Mum died prematurely, aged 68, in the year 1972, whilst her husband, my dad, lived on to 101, and did not die until 1999. I refer to her death as premature, because throughout her life she had a terrible primitive fear of surgery, and though it had been clear in the 1930's after my birth that she needed to go to hospital—to have some remedial internal operation, she was never prepared to do that.

Consequently, internal physical health problems developed over the years which steadily worsened, and which she took no action about, other than taking aspirins, and other pain-relief measures.

To sum up, I feel that Essie's life throughout, was a rather sad and unfulfilled one. She had some times of real joy, and other times of sadness, loneliness, and dissatisfaction. She was very much at home with her first son Con, when he was about, as they shared a lively and robust sense of humour, a naturally extrovert style, and excitement about many possibilities in the world. However, even in the good times, when we had holidays, or when times looked more encouraging economically, she was occasionally down, and low in spirit. Mum was a hard-working, loving, warm and caring person, who was surprisingly non-judgemental of others.

Despite the sadness in her life, I would like to pay tribute to her, because of the values which she passed on to her two sons, and which very much affected me. She had come to feel strongly against organised religion, as such, because of her father's hypocritical actions. Culturally though, she showed a great love of traditions in her cooking, and in many of her activities. What is important, is that she passed on the idea that you had to see people in a specific way. It was the case of not viewing people—as to whether they were black or white, nor whether they were of any particular race or religion, but what was important—she said and she saw, was that you had to see whether individuals were good and reasonable people, or whether they were untrustworthy, and essentially bad people. Perhaps, it is a somewhat simple construct, but it is one that had a deep affect upon me, and which I value, and for which I thank my sadly departed mother.

CHAPTER FIVE

The Wild Ones

As one travels around the world, you occasionally meet some extraordinary characters, who are larger than life. They are the confident, extrovert adventurers, who see the whole world as being their oyster. At best, they may turn out to be Hemingways or Steinbecks, but that is rarely the case.

Often such individuals are men, who have a strong belief in self, are self-centred, extrovert and great charmers. They are always ready to perform—in order to impress others, and are particularly concerned with the charming of strangers. The families from which such characters come however, may have mixed responses to them. Sometimes the families may be used, by such individuals. They are people who may form strong relationships, may take jobs and may get married, but they are not always there for the 'long run'. Thus divorces, sudden changes of country, or places where lived, and other unusual personal characteristics—may become evident. What is surprising is that there have been two such characters, or 'wild ones' in the Travis family. They are my father's brother Jack, in one generation, and my brother Conrad—in a second generation.

Jack's story has already been told in outline—he was born in 1899 in Leeds, and disappeared in 1924—on the borders of Canada and the United States. Perhaps the greater significance of his story, is the effect that he had unwittingly upon his nephew Conrad, who was born after he had disappeared. Jack, who was born in Leeds, was very anxious to get into the First World War, and (as far as I can make out), he volunteered early-on to go into the British army. However, he was not sent quickly to the front, and was anxious to get into the action. Somehow or other, he seemed to have then got into the Canadian army, and through being based with them, was sent to France. He was with the Canadian army fighting on the Western Front in France, when he was gassed. As a result of that gassing, Jack was sent back home for treatment and to recuperate. He appears to have been a much wilder and freer spirit than his brother Morris, who was always the steady and reliable elder brother. It seems that when he came back to Britain, he was not fit enough again to go back to fighting in France, and was not one to face the boredom of life as a civilian.

He thought that it was boring in the north of England. As soon as possible, he went over again to Canada, where he maintained very little contact with the family in England. It was very hard to get adequate information from my father, about what Jack did in North America, but piecing things together, it seems that as soon as the First World War was over, that very early on Prohibition was introduced in the United States—in post-War America. This is the sort of activity which created great opportunities for characters like the rather wild, charming, and adventurous Jack, who seems to have got into the game of whisky- and gun-running across the border between Canada and the United States, and as far as I could find out, he was doing this for some years!

My father had great difficulties trying to maintain contact with Jack in North America, so that the family here at home in the UK, knew that he was safe and well. It appears that very rarely did letters or information come from Jack in Canada or the United States, so that my father had to spend much time studying press articles, and trying to get other information. Dad was busy scanning Canadian newspapers, and contacting the Canadian Embassy, to find out where and what Jack was doing. The last news that the family had of Jack was in 1924, when Jack stated that all was going well, and a photo of him dressed rather like a Chicago gangster, was taken somewhere in Canada, and sent home in 1924. After that, despite enormous efforts on my father's part, the family was not able to find out anything more about Jack, and he disappeared completely, at that date.

Two years after Jack disappeared, my brother Con was born in Cardiff, Wales, in 1926. From the beginning of Con's story, he appears to have been a very lively, if not wild youngster, very free-spirited, and always up to mischief—as a very small boy. Apparently very early in life, Conrad learnt about his Uncle Jack, and became more and more interested in him, and seems to have treated him as almost a role model. He did not look to his father, Morris, for such a model, as he considered him rather dull in comparison to Uncle Jack. Early on, Con's story echoed the general family story—ie his early childhood and early schooling was in Cardiff, and then in 1939 when the family moved to New Zealand, he went with them. Finding himself in Wellington at the start of the Second World War, Conrad became very excited about the prospects of finding real interest in life, because a war had started! It is hard to know whether it is largely because of taking Jack as a role-model, or whether there was some genetic inheritance or not, that Con was very keen to replicate what his Uncle Jack had done, in the First World War.

From the time Con was 14, late in 1940, he pestered his parents that he was keen to join the forces and go overseas, but of course he was far too young to do so. He tried every rouse contacting the New Zealand Army, and then the Royal New Zealand Air Force, to see if it was possible to get into the armed forces. However, at 14 it was impossible to do so, even though he looked older than

Uncle Jack in the Canadian Army in World War I

Conrad in the New Zealand Army in World War II

his age. That did not stop Con from "hanging-out" with young soldiers, so that he was all the time, looking for an opportunity to get into the action. He would constantly say that he didn't want to miss out on the war, and he wanted to be out there in the fighting!

It must have been something like 1942, after the USA had entered the war, that US Marines and American G.I.'s first started appearing—in and around Wellington. Con immediately found opportunities to visit US bases, in and around the city. Very soon he was coming home on visits with GI's or U.S. marines, who would stay with us overnight. My mother became alarmed at how much time he was spending with these US soldiers, and wondered how much it was influencing him.

Then one day in either 1942 or 1943, Con disappeared! My mother was convinced that due to his friendship with all these American soldiers, that he must have joined them, boarded a troop-ship, and gone overseas. My father was cynical about this, but my mother was insistent, and after a week or two, with no sign of him, she insisted on going to visit the American Consul General in Wellington City Centre. I went with my mother to the Consul General's office. There, she stated to the Consul General that she was convinced that my brother had just gone on-board an American Troop-ship, and gone overseas. The Consul General stood up. He said "Madam, no-one can just walk on board an American Troop-ship!". However, my mother insisted that he was, somewhere in the Pacific, and she asked the Consul if he would make enquiries to help find him. It was four or five weeks before any news came through, as to what had happened to my brother, and during that time obviously my parents went through a period of enormous anxiety and worry. Then one day they had a phone-call, and I can't recall whether it was from the Consulate General, or from the American Embassy. It was to tell my parents that my brother was alive and well, and had been found fighting together with U.S. Marines, on the island of Guadalcanal, in the Solomon Islands, to the North of New Zealand. It seems that Con had been fighting with an Ack Ack Unit of the US Marines, on the American-held part of the island. There, one of the critical battles of the Pacific was taking place, and the Japanese were very strongly defending the island. Eventually, the Americans were able to fly him back to Wellington, and we then saw him—"full of beans", with a section of the wind-screen of a zero fighter, which his unit had shot down when he was on the island.

The most remarkable event, was when my mother insisted on him going to see the American Consul General in Wellington. There she took my brother, who told the Consul General, that yes—he had just put on Khaki relaxing clothes, and walked on-board an American Troop-ship! The Consul General visibly turned white, and had to sit down, to take-in this extraordinary information.

After this episode, when Con must have been something like 16 years old, he "couldn't be kept down", and was anxious to see how quickly he could get into either the New Zealand army or air force! At one stage he heard that there was an NZ expeditionary force, that was going to go through to Europe at that stage, and Con already had friends who were going to volunteer for it, and he wanted to go too. However, as he was under age, this required signatures from both my parents, and neither my father nor mother were prepared to give their signatures—to allow this. Several months later, when we heard that this expeditionary force was taking part in the severe fighting at Monte Casino in Italy, and suffered very, very high casualty rates, my brother was quiet for a week or two. He did eventually get into the army, and was part of the time with the New Zealand Army, before later transferring to the Royal New Zealand Air Force.

When the war finished, he went with the Royal New Zealand Air Force (RNZAF)—with its New Zealand Occupying Force, to Japan. There, Con was stationed at the air base at Iwakuni. This air base was near the destroyed city of Hiroshima, which had been devastated by one of the largest of the atomic bombs, near the end of the Second World War. He enjoyed his period with the RNZAF in Japan, getting involved in various exploits, getting to know some of the Americans based in the American Occupation Forces over there in Tokio, and from time to time sending us parcels, with all sorts of exotic things from Japan. Con used to be a sportsman, and was always keen to play football, or to go swimming. In Japan, he played in a New Zealand football team against American opponents. Later in life, he even played football in the Cardiff City Seconds team!

The war may have been over, but the story of Con's exploits does not end there. When in fact in 1946 the family had returned to England and Con was due for demobilisation, he decided he would come to England, as we were here. So, in Japan—he got a transfer to the RAF, so that he could be demobbed in England, rather than New Zealand. He eventually left Japan, sending home letters to my father, that he was probably coming with an amazing girl that he had met, and whom he was sure he would marry, whether dad liked it or not! We next heard from Hong Kong, where he was en route to Britain, but had met another woman, and was now going to marry her, having already dumped the first one—whom he had written about. When he arrived in England he had already separated from this latest girlfriend, but there were others between 1946 and 1951, when he conventionally married a girl from South Wales. His first wife Zelda, came from Porthcawl in South Wales. Resulting from that marriage, there was a little boy born at the very end of 1951, but though Con tried out various jobs, things were not going very well for him. After a few years Con & Zelda separated, and I think, were formally divorced, then he went off alone to Canada!

As this was not a time of Prohibition, there were no gun-running, or whisky-running opportunities in Canada. He seems to have gone through a range of jobs in Toronto, before he finally got to know the famous singer Connie Francis, whom he then joined—in her touring company, as a comedian! He then started touring with the Connie Francis Show, first in North America, and then in South Africa. It was when the show visited Johannesburg. possibly in 1963, that he then met an attractive South African woman, Ida, whom he married in that year. They had two sons in 1964, and 1966, living first in Johannesburg, then in Durban, and later returning to Jo'burg. Much to my surprise, Con—after marrying a South African wife, decided to stay in South Africa, because she was born there and didn't want to live anywhere else. This was the time of Apartheid in South Africa, and life was somewhat complex. However, Con made a career for himself there.

Con's sons—Steven and Linton, were brought up in South Africa, and it was there that Steven married a South African girl, and they had a baby daughter, after which Steven suddenly left South Africa, and arrived in England. We don't know the circumstances of his disappearance from South Africa, leaving his wife and small daughter behind, but in a very short time Con's son Steven was involved in a further two marriages to girls in Cornwall, and elsewhere in the South of England. My brother Con remained in South Africa, and now in 2012 aged 86, he is still living in Johannesburg. Con's wife Ida died a few years ago, but one of his sons, Linton, still lives in Johannesburg and Con seems to be working still, and having a busy and adventurous life in that country.

The story of having two 'wild ones' in the family, has an additional dimension to it. It is complex and difficult being one of two sons, when you are the younger one, and your big brother is some six years older, and happens to be the 'wild one'. As a youngster, one looks for guidance, friendship, understanding, and support from one's older brother. However, when you do not get it, you feel hurt, and rather let-down. Even 50 years on, Con refers to his younger brother as 'my kid brother'. Add to the story, that if one's brother also happens to be the first child, and the first grandchild in the family, then he always gets his way. If Con's father was reluctant to spoil him, he always found that the ever-present grandpa, would give him any cash, and anything else that he wanted.

Because my brother has been the 'wild one' in our generation, he was always off and "doing his own thing". So, by the time Con was 14, I found that it was important for me to try and find my own close friends, and I wasn't particularly looking for 'wild ones' like my brother, but people who could give companionship and friendship, that I had lacked, because my big brother was never about.

Fortunately, as I went into a young and idealistic profession, it attracted to it many lively people of quality and integrity, so I was fortunate that I could find people who could act as real friends. They compensated for the absent brother, who was always far more interested in being with and impressing his friends, and not really being interested in the family from which he came. My brother, as I said, lives in Johannesburg, and I live in Birmingham. That way, it more or less works in our relationship.

CHAPTER SIX

The Scottish Diaspora

Collin's English Dictionary defines the term 'Diaspora' in several ways. Firstly, it is given as "The dispersion of the Jews from Palestine after the Babylonian captivity", alternatively it gives "A dispersion or spreading, as a people originally belonging to one nation or having a common culture". Thus in addition to the commonly-used term 'Jewish Diaspora', one can equally refer to the Italian- , the Irish- , the Polish- , or Scottish-Diasporas. The Scottish Diaspora notably includes Canada, especially its provinces of British Columbia, Alberta and Nova Scotia, the United States of America, South Africa, Australia, and New Zealand. Of special importance in the New Zealand context, is the province of Otago, which was largely settled by Scots.

At secondary school in Wellington, namely Rongotai College, I was very aware of the Scots influence, as no less than 6 out of the 24 of the teaching staff in the 1940's were Scots, namely Messrs. Farquhar, Macaskill, McCaw, Fraser, Wilson and Kinross. The rigour, commitment, and strong identity of these Scots—very much influenced the character and feeling of the school, and one of them in particular, Mr Patrick Macaskill, was a very great influence upon me.

Pat Macaskill had a very specific background. His family had had to leave Stornoway in the Isle of Lewis, at a time of great unemployment and hunger, when a ship-load of people left the island for Nova Scotia in Canada. His family moved on from Nova Scotia to New Zealand, and that is where he was brought-up. He was responsible for the teaching of history, and of drama, and was an enormous influence upon the students who gained from his teaching. This was because of the quality of his knowledge, his personal character, his remarkable insights, and acting ability. He was a man who had a zest for knowledge, and the ability to communicate it to others, together with his strong sense of history, and of Scottish values. Sometimes when supposedly teaching Maori history, or the history of the Maori Wars, he would digress into the problems of 'the Highland clearances in Scotland', or tell us about the 'evils of absentee land-lordism'. In the drama group in particular, where we put on a number of productions, he was superb at helping students learn how to act, how to stage-produce, and how to present themselves on stage. Later, on New Zealand radio, he was to become the 'King of Quizzes,' because of his extraordinary knowledge of history, and he was to leave Rongotai later to become the director of the Regional Teachers Training College for the Wellington Region, at Trentham.

The academic philosophy of Rongotai is of much interest. The school was originally started off by a core of staff, notably including the Headmaster Fritz Martin Renner, and the Scots Mr Farquhar. They had come from Wellington College, and brought with them, traditional academic rigour, and an innovative framework. Martin's 2003 Book gives a fuller description of this phase. Their approach to academic content was Geddesian in character. Professor Patrick Geddes, of Edinburgh, had related study focus to ideas of 'Folk, Work, and Place'. Thus, early on in studies, pupils would learn about their local environment—where people lived, and how and where they worked. From the local, one progressed to the regional, then the national, and finally to the international scales. Site visits thus went from local factories, right up to seeing Parliament—which functions in their home-city, and go on national visits that included a climbing-trip to Mt. Cook-the highest mountain in New Zealand!

Though—over time, the school was streamed—in terms of academic quality, into 'a' and 'b' streams, this was balanced-up by devoting a full afternoon per week to 'clubs.' which one could choose to join. Thus one could choose to join activities such as drama, sport, or music. One had the freedom to develop strong personal interests, and skills, in a significant block of time. I was fortunate enough to choose 'Drama' for a 3 hour period, and learned an enormous amount, under Macaskill's brilliant tutelage. One learned about theatre, communication, stagecraft, production, voice control, and presentation. It was an unexpected aspect of Rongotai College, that gave one all the key skills needed for potential academics, actors, and lawyers! Furthermore, the close personal, and informal working with a really creative mind like Pat's, was an educational boost unlikely to be repeated in one's life!

Many years later I was to meet him again during a visit to New Zealand, and was surprised and delighted to find that he was still a young, vigorous man, with a new second wife, and was someone who immediately inspired confidence, and openness, when you met him. I will always be grateful to this

The Scottish staff at Rongotai College, in New Zealand
were the influential quarter of the total, 1946.

inspiring teacher; it is his influence which stood me in so much good stead, later in my life.

Patrick was perhaps characteristic of the best of these educational influences that one had from Scots', and other specific migrant groups in New Zealand. The culture, the sporting impacts, and the many ways in which these various Diasporas, affected an immigrant society like New Zealand, was very noticeable. You were aware in each New Zealand city of the Caledonian Societies, but also of the Welsh Societies and the Welsh Choirs. Burns Nights, which one became familiar with in New Zealand, prepared one for the experience of Burns Nights later—in Scotland, England, and elsewhere in the world. One finds that whether in Hong Kong, or Jerusalem—they are celebrated with great gusto!

Otago is a very special case—within the Scottish Diaspora. It is a "little Scotland away from Scotland". It is a province largely settled by Scots, and is renowned for the quality of its University in Dunedin, whose buildings are modelled on those of Glasgow University.

Dunedin itself, meaning the 'new Edinburgh', is laid out with some of the character of the new town of Edinburgh, and has so many Scots street-names within it, that one could imagine one is in Scotland. The Province has remarkable educational achievements, in addition to having Highland Games, and so many other cultural features that you would expect to find in a little Scotland remote from Scotland!

One cannot but help comment upon the creative impact of specific migrant groups in New Zealand. We lived in Wellington, where my parents belonged to the Welsh Society, and sang in its choir. It was a vigorous and lively organisation, that added to the vitality of life in the city. One was also aware of a small number of Greek families—who sent their children to Maris Brothers Schools, and that anglicised their names so that the 'Georgiardis' family became the 'George family', and so on. In Wellington there was a small Italian community, and Italians had been the first people to settle in the suburb of Island Bay. In fact, it was Italian fishing boats that one could still see in the 1940's, moored out in the Bay—enclosed by its protective island. Another very large migrant group from diverse places, was the Polynesian community, which was drawn from many Pacific islands, and had settled in large numbers in the City of Wellington (see Ombler,1999). This was because of its port's international accessibility, and the pull of its governmental and administrative functions. There are today something like 35,000 Polynesians living in Wellington itself! Since the 1840's, when there was an original Maori settlement in the heart of Wellington, the Maori community has moved up the coast. They are now concentrated in two places, about 30 miles away, in the city in Porirua, and nearby Titahi Bay. The character of Wellington—both physical and social, is well shown in Graham Stewart's book of 2010.

Living in and with the Scots Diaspora, enabled one to gain an understanding of Scottish identity, and respect for the values and traditions of Scottish society. Thus it was that life in New

Zealand, very much prepared me ultimately for life and work in Scotland! When we first came to the UK in 1946, I was always aware of Scots whom I met. Though this was not a notable feature in Cardiff, it was something that I became very aware of, when working in Basildon, and Birmingham, before going to Edinburgh. When I married in 1957, I found that my wife had a Scottish grandfather, and through him, and his Scots relatives, this gave us a further link to Scotland as well. We went to Tobermory, on the Isle of Mull, for our Honeymoon, and once again I found I was totally at home in such an environment, with people of such values.

Our Kiwi friends—John and Judy Stewart, at their farm in Feilding, North Island, New Zealand, 1998.

It is notable that I have known no less than three people with the name 'John Stewart'. The first was a Scots architect, with whom I worked in Basildon New Town, the second was a New Zealand Scot from Otago, who was a student of mine in Edinburgh, and who later worked with me in Birmingham. When we eventually settled in

Birmingham, and I was working at Birmingham University, my fellow professor in the same building, was yet another John Stewart, who was the distinguished Professor of Local Government Studies! Life in the New Zealand Diaspora, thus gave me a preparation not only for a time of living in Scotland, but a natural affinity with Scots, whom I was to meet in the rest of my life. Having been given a 'radical Scots education' in the Scottish Diaspora, it was extremely easy to understand Scottish attitudes, values, prejudices, when later we were working, and living in Edinburgh. I have a personal debt both to the Scottish Diaspora, and to Scotland, and I found it was an absolute privilege and delight—to spend some eight years working and living in Edinburgh itself, having been prepared for it—by my time in New Zealand!

My upbringing in the Scottish Diaspora prepared me for that later life in Scotland, where Geddes had lived and worked. There I had the chance to take a small and almost dead old planning school, re-invigorate it, build up its staff, human and technical resources, twice re-house it, develop both undergraduate and postgraduate courses, and build-up a doctoral programme. All was possible in the 1960's, in a confident Scottish homeland that believed in education! There I saw and guided Doctoral theses done by people like Michael Affolter and Veronica Burbridge. So much happened in those eight years in Edinburgh, that it was for me like a full, and fulfilling life in Scotland.

CHAPTER SEVEN

World Sea Travel
and the Global Village

World travel by sea between distant nations such as United Kingdom and Australia or New Zealand, was the norm until the 1950's. The advantages of these journeys were that they gave all the passengers time to adapt to the changes of place, the changes of weather, the changes of climate, and even the changes of season, in the course of the long sea journeys. The disadvantage was of course the amount of time taken, as whilst those going on a major holiday—with plenty of time to spare—would enjoy such a long sea trip, or indeed those migrating would equally do so. However, for business men, or anyone constrained in the amount of time available, such trips were very demanding in terms of time used. It was not until the 1960's with changes in aircraft use and in pricing, that this all changed. Since then one has lost the advantage of these long sea journeys, but the changeover to large-scale, long-haul air travel, has meant that the time of travel between distant countries has been so reduced that the apparent size of the globe has been reduced accordingly.

Large numbers of people are now travelling long distances across the globe, in relatively short times, for example it now takes less than 24 hours to fly from Britain to New Zealand, and less than 20 hours to fly to Australia from the UK. Such reductions in travel time have reduced the apparent size of the globe, and have created for frequent world-travellers, a global village in which contacts can often be easily made face to face, in the course of less than 24 hours. Our world journeys by sea in 1939 from Britain to New Zealand, and in 1946 from New Zealand to the UK were fortunate pieces of timing in two senses. The first was the opportunity to see the condition of the world in the months leading up to the Second World War, and the second—allowing an early opportunity to cross the globe under post-war peace conditions.

As already indicated earlier, the 1939 journey started at London's Port of Tilbury, when we boarded the large Orient liner, the S.S. Orford. We were to be on board this ship for some four weeks, until we left it at Sydney, in New South Wales. The journey was a rich and memorable one, as there were many of call, and very strong impressions given which remain with me till today—some 73 years later! My first recollection is when the ship was making its way through the Bay of Biscay, where for the first time we experienced fairly rough sea conditions. My father and I were fortunate in that we had quickly got our sea-legs, and enjoyed this rougher sea weather. Unfortunately—my mother, grandpa and brother, found it much more difficult, and did not have a very enjoyable time passing through the Bay of Biscay.

Our first port of call was Gibraltar, where we left the ship in small boats, in order to land at the port. This was memorable as from time to time the boats would be slightly lifted into the air by large fish surfacing, and I'm still not sure whether these were porpoises, sharks or whatever! Gibraltar itself as the first foreign port of call seemed very disappointing, rather domestic in scale, and the only really memorable thing was the size of the rock and the sight of the Barbary Apes encountered higher up on the rock. After leaving Gibraltar, we entered the Mediterranean, the sea was much calmer, conditions suddenly became much warmer and friendlier, and as we had several ports of call in the Mediterranean, this was a very memorable part of the journey.

S. S. Wanganella, 1939

From the UK to NZ on the S. S. Orford

The second port of call was Toulon, which is on the south coast of France, and is not far from Nice. What was extraordinary about that port was that almost all of the French battle fleet was assembled there, and it provided an incredible impression for those on any visiting passenger ships at the time. I was to remember later, when France was defeated by Germany in the war, that this was the battle-fleet which scuttled itself in that port, but of course when we saw it, it was looking in great shape.

After Toulon, the ship moved on to the port of Naples, or Napoli, where we had a further stop. My main recollection is that of seeing Mount Vesuvius, and of there being a funicular railway which went up the mountain. However, other than remembering that I felt hot and tired, and was having difficulty coping with the heat, Naples was not particularly memorable. What I do recall is that at Naples quite a number of German refugees from Nazism boarded the ship. They were making their way as immigrants to Australia, and later-on board the ship, I recall meeting the children of a family whose surname was Birnbaum, with whom I spent some time. These German children spoke no English, and obviously at that stage I spoke no German! However, we got to know each other by sharing certain songs, which we sang from Hansel and Gretel, which they knew in German, and I knew in English, so in that way we learned some basic vocabulary from each other.

It was a few days before we reached our next port of call, which was a very different place, namely Port Said, at the entrance to the Suez Canal. This was our first taste of the Arab World. There, the bright light, hot sunshine, different architecture, different and pungent smell, and feel of the place, made it seem very exotic. What was special for us was that it was there—at Port Said, that we were to meet my mother's brother—who is my Uncle Max, who was coming to see us from British Mandatory Palestine. Much to my surprise, he had come by train, on what was then the Palestine Mandatory

Government Railways—which offered a train journey between Tel Aviv and Port Said. The train had come over the swing bridge at Kantara, and I recall that my uncle was waiting for us on the quayside in the port. It was exciting to meet this unknown uncle, in this exotic port, and I seem to recall we all went out to lunch or tea somewhere, but I cannot recall whether my aunt was there, or not. All too quickly we had to board the ship again, and then we entered the Suez Canal.

The Suez Canal was a great surprise, for it seemed like an engineered, very busy, blue road, full of shipping, cutting its way through the heart of the desert. One was surprised to see, despite all the shipping in front and behind us, that on both sides of the canal, there seemed to be nothing other than empty desert, with sand glistening in the sun. When eventually we came to the south end of the Canal, there was another port, namely Suez, but we stopped only briefly there, before the ship made its way on down the Red Sea.

We had now moved into the Tropics and the Mediterranean warmth gave way to the blinding light and heat of the tropical Red Sea. We seemed to move slowly southward, until we arrived at the Port of Aden, in the Yemen. In those days Aden was a British protectorate, and so when we went ashore, everything was relatively easy, as one was dealing with customs and officialdom in English, and not some exotic language. The strongest memory for me from that port of call was our visit to a strange park, on the edge of the town. The park had an enormous bowl in it—hundreds of feet across, and when one came to the edge of it and looked down, the whole bowl was full of snakes—writhing in their hundreds or thousands, within this area. It was a fascinating, repulsive, and totally hypnotic experience, which I remember vividly to this day.

There was more time at sea before next we reached Colombo, the port and capital of what was then the Island of Ceylon, and which is now Sri Lanka. We seemed to have had a number of adventures in that port, where taxi drivers attempted to take us away from the destinations which we had asked for, to all sorts of strange native destinations! However, we did eventually finish up at a hotel, which had been recommended to us as a place to go for either lunch or tea, and I remember sitting on a terrace verandah, and there taking tea, and looking out through sunglasses, at the exotic vegetation, and the sparkling sea in the distance.

After Ceylon, there was a long sea crossing through to Australia, and it was a source of great interest and surprise to find ourselves arriving at Port Fremantle—the Port for Perth, in Western Australia. Though here again we were in a Mediterranean-type climate, what was surprising and delightful, was that the place was so English! The men were dressed in white shorts and white hats, the shopping centre seemed to be incredibly English, and the choice of fruits, goods, and everything—reminded one of very warm summer conditions somewhere in the south of England. We explored both the port and the city of Perth and we, like all passengers on board who were travelling further on, found Perth a delightful first taste of Australia.

The ship stopped at three further Australian ports, first at the port of Adelaide, where we spent something like a half-day, then on to Melbourne, and finally to Sydney—which was the ship's destination. For us, the most important stop was that at Melbourne, because there we were able to meet my mother's second brother, my Uncle Reuben, with his Australian wife, and their young son, who was a couple of years younger than myself. They lived in St. Kilda, in an affluent part of inner Melbourne, and were welcoming, as well as showing us around what seemed to be a large and attractive city. However, when we did get to Sydney, we found that we had arrived in the great Australian metropolis, and as one came into that wonderful harbour, and saw the famous so-called 'coat hanger' bridge, one had memorable impressions of a great waterfront city. This was, of course, in the days before the Opera House existed, and before the multiple skyscrapers clustered on the Sydney Cove waterfront. However, it was an extremely attractive and impressive port city destination, and one which later I was to enjoy visiting again.

After a few days in Sydney, we were once again boarding a ship, this time the S.S. Wanganella, for our four day sea journey across the Tasman Sea, to Wellington in New Zealand. We had mixed weather and sea conditions, in the crossing of the Tasman Sea. Of course, when we arrived in Wellington, we were greeted by all of the family, my father's two brothers and their wives and children! There were complex and mixed impressions in the first few days in what was a very different, and much smaller port city, but all on a wonderful harbour, contained by high hills, and distant snow-covered mountains. We had arrived in New Zealand, and we thought that this was going to be our permanent home.

New Zealand is an island-nation, and though its land area is slightly larger than that of the United Kingdom, it is a much longer and narrower country, which extends over a thousand miles in length. It is made up of three islands, and going from north to south, these are—the North Island, the South Island, and then to the south of South Island—a much smaller island called Stewart Island. In 1940 only about 3 million people lived in New Zealand. In the 1940's we had two opportunities for sea travel within New Zealand, one during war-time, travelling to Picton, in the Marlborough Sounds, and once in the post-war period, going further south to Port Lyttleton, for Christchurch. As mentioned earlier, we travelled on the S.S. Tamahine to Picton, and though that journey only takes three or four hours from Wellington, it is an interesting one, as you pass through the vast expanses of Wellington harbour, then go out into the very exposed Cook Strait, and finally cruise in through the Sounds to Picton. Those Sounds are a lovely area of flooded valleys, with bush covered hills, and only a few occasional small settlements, scattered around these expansive waterways.

The longer sea journey later on, was on board the S.S. Rangatira, which is an overnight journey, as the trip took about twelve hours. One had the experience of having family cabins on the ship, and having both supper and breakfast on board, for this long sea journey before one arrived at the small port in the Banks Peninsula, and travelled on by public transport into Christchurch. Christchurch is the most English of New Zealand cities, and before its sad devastation in the recent major earthquake, was one of the most attractive cities in the Southern hemisphere. Christchurch, with its tree-lined roads and parks, is crossed by the winding River Avon, and at the centre of the city its monumental public buildings are in stone, neo-gothic in character, and very much echo the architecture of a number of English cities. It was a beautiful, easy-going and attractive city to visit, with many attractions for visitors ranging from its shopping centres and museums, through to its very fine beaches and parks.

1946 was of course the big sea trip from New Zealand to Britain. On this journey we travelled across the Pacific, and came via the Panama Canal and the United States, on via the Atlantic to the UK. Conditions in 1946 were very different to those in 1939. First of all the ship that we went on, the S.S. Akaroa, was an old ship which I think New Zealand had got from Germany or Italy after the war, and made a member of one of its main shipping lines. It was a nice old ship, much smaller than the Orford, which had probably been over 20,000 tonnes, whereas this ship was about 14,000 tonnes, but was a very sea-worthy old vessel. The passengers were very different too, for whereas on the Orford going to Australia there were still many emigrants going out to live in the Dominions in 1939, in 1946 the largest block of passengers, were New Zealand women who had married GIs, or US marines. They were going on this sea journey to the State of Virginia, where they were to enter the United States.

The sea journey across the Pacific was not very notable, other than for the fact of visiting one island, called Henderson Island, which was not inhabited—other than by a very large colony of rats. Fortunately we did not go ashore, and hopefully part of the rat population was not able to board the ship at that stage! After a long time at sea, with the full heat and warmth of the Pacific, we at last arrived at the Panama Canal. This was a very different experience to seeing the Suez Canal. The Panama Canal is an extraordinary man-engineered canal that links the oceans via a series of large lakes and canal stretches. Because of the difference in sea-levels at the two sides of the Isthmus, there are huge locks at a series of points in the canal, and even large ships have to enter these locks, and be elevated or lowered, to the changed levels, to pass through the canal.

There are two ports—at the two ends of the canal, namely Panama City at one end, and the Port of Colon at the other. Neither of these cities were terribly interesting, nor was the passage through the canal itself. What one was aware of was the lush tropical jungle coming right down to the water's edge, and one could see from the ship the extraordinary richness of coloured birds flying about amongst the trees, and crocodiles or alligators, which would launch themselves from the water's edge, out towards the ship, in a rather menacing way!

Tropical showers would strike the ship, like moving walls of water, and soon after a cauldron of steam would arise from the decks!

The two most interesting ports of call on this trip were Curacao and Newport News. First of all, after we had crossed the Caribbean, we went to the Port of Willemstad, at Curacao, in the Dutch Antilles. This was a very exotic port and town, with wonderful, colourful, Dutch colonial architecture, painted buildings, a mixture of white Dutch colonials, and lively black local people on the streets, with traffic moving at a hair-raising speed. Vehicles just about missed hitting the goats, and other animals, that seem to wander across the roads on the island. The Port is lively, interesting, exotic, friendly, and one of the most interesting places one can visit, in the course of world travels.

The second place, which was very, very different, was a week or two later, when the ship arrived in the United States, travelling up the Chesapeake Bay, to the Port of Newport News, in Virginia. Here we stopped for a few days, because of the landing of the large number of New Zealand G.I. brides, and thus there was a chance to not only explore the town of Newport News, but even go across to the state capital of Richmond, in Virginia. Going to the shops in Newport News was a curious experience, because one had the first contact with small-town America—a quaintly naive and rather suspicious environment. When they asked in the shops where we had come from, and we said New Zealand, they wanted to know where that was in relation to Hollywood! Shops were full of goods, and one was given a strange first impression of popular '40s American culture—with all the milk bars, cheap shops, large scale car ownership, even then, and the strange feeling of this old—new country, that is the State of Virginia, in the East of the United States.

After a long and not very satisfactory crossing of the North Atlantic in mixed weather conditions, we eventually arrived at the Port of Southampton, which still looked rather grey and battered, in the early post-war period. There was still evidence of war damage, there was a greyness and some buildings even still had blackout on them in 1946. We suddenly felt we had left young, lively, relatively affluent New Zealand, and had come to a large, old, grey and tired country, struggling to get itself together, after all of the ravages of a major World War, which had hit those at home, as much as the troops, who had gone overseas.

To continue the saga of sea travel, but for a ferry crossing in 1951 to France when I went with a school friend on a hitchhiking trip around France, it was not until 1953 that I was again to go on a sea-going liner—this time to Spain.

Sea travel by passenger ships has been a source delight throughout my life, and this applied in the 1950's as much as in 1940's, and even later as well. In 1953 I had to go to Spain, where as part of my learning of Spanish language at Manchester University, I needed to take a summer course at Santander, in the north of that country. In order to do this, I went via the port of Tilbury where I caught the Royal Mail Line's S.S. Andes, which was basically an immigrant ship, taking Portuguese and Spanish migrants to South America. What I discovered in 1953, was that on the ship's three-day journey to Vigo in Spain, it was virtually empty, and one could get a single fare there for only £11! Other people too discovered there was this easy and cheap option to go on the Andes to Spain! These were places that were taken up by artists, poets, students going to study, and anyone other than impoverished immigrants to South America! It was a great three-day sea journey, with very interesting travel companions, and extraordinary to arrive in 1953 at the Port of Vigo, in the time of Franco's Fascist Rule. There were no cars in the streets of the port, the city looked poverty-stricken. It was dominated by a skyscraper hospital with fascist slogans on it, and we discovered that the top five storeys could not be used, because of various problems in the building. Legless beggars were crawling on the streets of Vigo in 1953, and they were being covered with droppings from passing horses. The lack of restaurants meant that to get a meal one went down to the waterfront, into a working quarter, where there were bodegas or caves. There you could sit and wait until freshly caught sardines were thrown into barrels of boiling oil, and then eat the freshly cooked sardines, with hunks of bread, and drink bowls of Ribeiro white wine! It was a different world.

In 1954 there was a further opportunity for sea travel, when I went as a Manchester University student, on a student work scheme to Israel. In those days one had to take the train to the English Channel, cross by ferry, and then take the train to Paris, get a connecting train in Paris through to Marseille. In Marseille one had to wait for the steamers of the Zim-Shoham Shipping Line, which had shipping services between Marseille and Israel. In those days, the five-day sea journey seemed the only realistic travel option. Journeys outwards on the S.S. Jerusalem and the return journey on the S.S. Artsa—are journeys which I will write more about in another chapter.

In the 1950's and '60's there were many opportunities for shorter sea journeys, such as sea ferry crossings to and from France, and to Belgium, and Holland. One slightly longer sea journey was once on holiday, and once on work—going across to Denmark. The oddest trip was on the sea journey by the Olsen Line, from Newcastle upon Tyne to Bergen, in Norway. That was because it happened to be on Norway's National Day, and all the passengers and crew seemed to be continually drunk!

One of the most interesting journeys was in 1962, in early days of our married life, when my wife and I took our one and a half year old daughter with us on a Polish freighter to Gdansk. This was a journey which lasted several days across the North Sea, went on through the Kiel Canal, and on via the Baltic to Gdansk. There were only some 12 passengers on board the ship, but it was an interesting journey, as one got to know the other passengers as well as some of the crew. One was limited in one's movement, as timber was tied on the decks, and there was very little area to move about, on board the ship. The Polish holiday is something that will be referred to elsewhere in this book.

By the 1960's fewer passenger shipping lines existed, and increasingly if you wanted sea journeys, then only sea-cruises were available, the like of which did not appeal to my wife and myself. Ultimately, air travel gradually overtook passenger sea travel for medium and long haul world travel.

The last two memorable sea-journeys which my wife and I experienced were: a return holiday sea-trip by Brittany Ferries

Ltd. from Plymouth in England to Santander (Spain), and our one and only sea-cruise, on board the S.S.Discovery, taking a 13 day trip to and from Baltic ports, with St. Petersburg (Russia) as the ultimate destination. This cruise included port stops at Copenhagen, (Denmark), Stockholm, (Sweden), Talinn, (Estonia), St Petersburg—Russia (2.5 day visit), Gdynia-Gdansk (Poland), to a former DDR port, and the Kiel Canal. It was a medium-sized ship—with perhaps 300 passengers on board, so one did not get overwhelmed with people, as on a larger vessel with thousands of passengers aboard. What was frustrating for us was that the ship paid visits of less than a day, to all ports, other than St Petersburg. This meant that every shore trip was perforcedly very superficial, even when one knew the specific destination in advance. Port cities can be lively and varied places, and each needs several days to explore seriously. Thus sea-cruising, with its superficiality, is simply not for us.

My work-life since the 1960's has involved frequent air travel. This has enabled getting to many destinations—long, medium and short-haul, fairly quickly and effectively. The personal experience of passing through airports, being 'processed', and then travelling by air, is one that has become steadily more debased, over time. Mass-travel has meant that handling capacity is often stretched to the limit. Personalised service on-flight, is now only a reality when travelling first class, or on business class flights, when they are under-used. When you are conscious of the impacts of air travel upon the host environment, you are increasingly reluctant to choose this travel mode. However, with time constraints upon work schedules, the air travel option is often the only possibility on offer! Air travel has been vital for me, on work-trips to places like Hong Kong, the Maldives, Australia, the USA, Canada, the Canaries, Algeria, Albania, Norway, and various East European and Mediterranean destinations.

When, all too rarely, the time available and route has permitted, a road travel option has been possible, and has been taken. This travel is so much richer than air travel, eg driving from Scotland to Poland, or to the former Federal Yugoslavia. When there have not been intervening seas, long-distance rail travel, for example from Hook van Holland to Poland, during the Cold War, had extra dimensions of interest, and excitement, that air travel rarely offers!

Today, life in the Global Village, depends upon frequent and convenient air travel supplementing other forms of communication that do not involve—one's physical movement abroad. Aircraft technology has to be improved and made "greener" quickly. The rate of environmental damage by man, gives no choice. The benefits of this air-travel based Global Village, are spelt out elsewhere in this book. Professional and personal links globally, cannot be maintained adequately without such occasional face to face meetings. Skype and tele-conferencing have their uses, but are a poor second best, in this context.

I am grateful that because of the timing of major travel in my life, that long sea journeys by passenger ships did take place, and were so enriching for me. Some rail and road journeys, especially driving for a month in the Canadian Rockies, were truly memorable and special. However, the two world-crossing sea-journeys—were for me the ultimate travel experiences.

CHAPTER EIGHT

Explorations of Youth

The period from 1946 to 1951 really divides up into two phases, namely the transitional or traumatic changeover period from 1945 to 1947, and then secondly—the 1948 to 1951 phase, which was a time of the explorations of youth.

The trauma of changeover is referred to, because it is felt I had left behind close family, friends, a plentiful supply of food and clothing in New Zealand, and relative prosperity, in exchange for the unknown. What I had hoped for was the excitement and interest of change, namely going to a different and new country, as far as I was concerned, moving to what was expected to be a welcoming family, and to people whom I thought would be friendly. However, much to my surprise and disappointment, when we got here to the UK, what I found was a grey, blitzed and blighted country, of tired people, who were still suffering from the after-effects of war. In Cardiff, the trams still had their wartime blackouts on their windows, utility furniture was on sale, and food was rationed, as was clothing. When we went into our first restaurant in London, the only meat available was horse meat. Some of the family met were unwelcoming, and there were many things which were a source of major adjustment. The fact that I had 'a funny accent', led to my being treated as a stranger and foreigner, in the country in which I had been born! Great Britain in 1946 was a land of shortages and austerity, and what was overwhelming was the daily and frequent contrasts, and let-downs of life here, compared to the life in New Zealand. Socially I found that the 'Brits' were much more formal than the relaxed Kiwis, and whether in terms of the economy, domestic arrangements, or cultural affairs, simply everything was different, and took quite a lot of adjustment to accept.

There were all sorts of transitional problems, both in 1946 and 1947. In 1946 after we had first come here, I had the terrible continuing problem of a serial dream. During the day I was living in Wales, but at night time when I went to sleep, my life in New Zealand continued in my dreams, and this is something I had to go and see a doctor about. The doctor stated that this was a fairly natural response, provided it did not last more than three months, or if it did last longer than that—it might require some psychiatric treatment. Fortunately, just before the three months were up, this process of dreams stopped. Perhaps I was adjusting to being in this very different place.

The winter in early 1947, did not help. I was not used to extreme weather conditions, and the great snows and cold of that winter, created many problems. On one occasion when I went off to Llandaff, I got caught in a snow drift in the fields near the cathedral, and had to be dragged out, as I was simply not used to snow. Another big changeover was when at last I started at school. The differences between schooling in the two countries were enormous. In New Zealand, everyone was called by their first name, and the atmosphere was very warm, relaxed, and open. Here in Cardiff, in an academically rigorous grammar school, one had to get used to being called by one's surname, and also adjust to the formality of the whole system.

Three key personal teenage elements: the bike-for freedom, the folk dance display in the 1951 Festival of Britain, and the Town Planning Model that won the School Competition.

Staff and students spoke in a very different style, and there were new subjects with which one had to cope. I was suddenly thrown into physics and geometry, which were totally new to me, and in the subjects that were familiar, like French and Latin, I had to adjust to being very backward, because the students here were years ahead of us. Thus in all these circumstances, I missed my old friends from Rongotai College on the one hand, and the close family that I'd left behind in Wellington. Very soon, I wished we had not come to the UK.

There was so much to adjust to in terms of content, and standards at the school, that for the first time ever—I had to drop a year in my schooling, and it was very frustrating to drop back a year, as I'd always been among the higher performing students in the 'A' Stream at my old school. However, at last in 1947, I started to make new friends at school, boys like Terry Dalby, David Ainsworth and David Hine. Terry was the illegitimate son of an English Lord, and had not previously found a soul mate at school, so he was particularly welcoming. One night Terry borrowed a tent, which we erected in his garden. We spent the night in it, and had a midnight barbecue of sausages and baked beans! David Ainsworth came from a very formal, middle-class background, but was ready to talk and go on trips together. David Hine was the son of the head of the Welsh National Music College, and was intellectually lively, and was something of a loner, so he was keen to go for walks and talks. A lively pair in the class were Kennedy and White, who were often the cause of much laughter. A little later, I became very friendly with another of the boys who was also focused on geography, namely Keith Thomas, and that friendship did start to develop when I got a bike. As I got to know others in the class, exchanges of ideas, and the gradual blossoming of friendship, started to make life in Cardiff look rather better than it had—up till then.

For years I had wanted a bicycle, but because of my mother's reactions to my brother Con and his wildness, she had been somewhat restrictive and safeguarding of her second son. Thus she had prevented me from getting a bike, for years. The battle to get a Roadster was at last won when I was 16, and this changed life very fundamentally. Getting a bike meant personal freedom, and though I was not allowed to get a sports-bike, at least getting a Raleigh Roadster, made sure that I could get out, and about, able to join other friends on their bike-trips as well.

What was very special about this early post-war period, was that one had the freedom of fairly empty roads, both in parts of the city, and especially in the countryside, when one went further afield. It was a time when there were virtually no private cars—of course it was before motorways in the UK, and nearly everyone did their main travel by train, or bus. Thus having a bike, gave one the freedom to roam over the Counties of Glamorgan and Monmouthshire. This meant that one could go off either by one-self, cycling on a free afternoon or free day, or go with one of one's school friends, to interesting places where you could sit, have a picnic, or just chat, and talk about life. One only needed to go about 12 or 13 miles from home, westward from Cardiff in the Cowbridge direction, to find the little village of Bonvilston, and about half a mile north of it the area called Welsh St. Donats. This was a stretch of over a mile of attractive woodland with walks, lakes, and great quiet places to sit, and think, or socialise with friends. On several occasions I cycled with friends from Cardiff High to this woodland, which became one of my favourite spots to the west of Cardiff.

However, one had quite a choice of places to visit, because further to the west—were the great sand dunes of Merthyr Mawr. These great sand dunes were like a miniature Sahara, and in fact were used by British film-makers as sets for desert films! Alternatively, going on trips of 20 to 25 miles out in the east and north east directions from Cardiff, one could get to the beautiful Wye Valley, and explore interesting places like Raglan, with its ruined castle, Caerleon with its Roman town, and the small Monmouthshire villages and hills.

Unlike my brother—with his love of football and swimming, my passions soon turned out to be cycling, walking, hill-walking and climbing, things that I could either do alone, or ideally with one other friend. There were two favourite long walks in Cardiff—either in Roath Park with its long boating lake, or in Bute Park which had been the extensive grounds of the Bute Castle, which had now been gifted to the people of the city, and had now become Cardiff Castle. Alternatively, one could cycle to the Penarth Waterfront, and sit on the pebbles of the beach there, and watch passing shipping going into and out of the Port of Cardiff. Another great place to go to was just to the north of Cardiff, to the magical fairytale castle of Castell Coch. This had been a folly built by the Bute's for their escape from the city, and the docks, and all those things that had created the Bute family's wealth—associated with the coal industry, and the shipping trade.

In this period I found that life was dividing up into segments, because I was doing different things with different groups of people. When I was with my non-Jewish school friends, we spent times going off in pairs—that is two boys together, on cycle-trips, where we explored life and ideas. One found that slowly—after being a stranger, one was accepted, and made new friends. On the other hand, I had joined a youth organisation, which was for both boys and girls, and that felt much more normal than this male only life, within single sex secondary schools. The organisation that I joined was one that I had known in New Zealand, and it is called Habonim. This is a Socialist, Zionist organisation, with strong affinities to the scouting movement, it involves camping, going off on big hikes in the countryside, singing around bonfires, and other scouting activities. In this context, the family was still known locally from pre-war days, and therefore I was more readily accepted than I had been as a stranger in the school setting. What was great too was that I particularly enjoyed this outdoor life, the pioneer work and digging the ditches, making the latrines, carrying lamps, walking through the night across the hills, it all appealed enormously. In addition too, we tended to pair off with girlfriends, and it all felt more normal than just being in an all-male environment at school. I became a youth leader over time, and organising programmes and activities was challenging fun! One weekend in May 1948, we were at a rambling camp in the Welsh Hills, when someone, with a miniature radio, which could get long wave, enabled us to hear the announcement of the creation of the State of Israel! A magical and memorable moment!

Some of my lifelong friendships date from this period, such as with Keith Thomas, whom I started going out with on short cycle rides in the Wentloog area, an area of reclaimed low marshes at the east of Cardiff. Also there was 'Bimbo' Jessel, who was one of the youth leaders in Habonim. I still see Keith and his wife Tonie occasionally nowadays, though as they live down in the Isle of Wight, it's much more difficult to get together now. Bimbo died a couple of years ago, in rural Cambridgeshire, after having lived on kibbutz, been an economic consultant in Switzerland, Jamaica, and various places in Africa!

One of the delights of this time, in addition to general social life, and starting to find girlfriends, was the beginnings of intellectual exploration as well. Only a few hundred yards away from Cardiff High School, was a local shopping centre—called Clifton Street, and on that street was a small shop owned by my mum's Uncle Sam and Aunty Rae. These were the lovely Jackson couple, who long ago had been welcoming to my mother, when she had first gone to Birmingham in her youth, and now were extremely welcoming and friendly relatives for me in Cardiff. Sam was a big hulk of a man, looking rather like a Russian peasant, but with some scars on his head caused by a railway accident in which he had been, in his youth. Rae was a lovely bubbly soul, who always put the kettle on—the moment you came into sight, and would go and get her store of special biscuits, which she would bring out as well! She suffered from anaemia, and had constant nose bleeds, but looked after Uncle Sam and visitors like myself, as though it was one of the great delights in her life. Sam was a natural intellectual, who had never had a proper education, but was self-educated, and had a zest for reading and knowledge. As a book-lover, and great user of the local library, he would always have a new book for me, when I would pop in—possibly at lunchtime, to see them. One day he would enthuse about Sinclair Lewis, and would recommend the book 'Main Street' to me, or more exciting still Arthur Koestler's new book—'Thieves in the Night'. These sort of recommendations from Uncle Sam, supplemented David Hine's recommendation of 'The Journal of a Disappointed Man' by Barbellion, which was a great source of interest. My own library explorations took in Steinbeck, Hemmingway, and Huxley, whilst more and more I delved into the philosophy and planning ideas of Lewis Mumford, Patrick Geddes, and Abercrombie. It was a time of special joy in reading books, because though there was radio, there was no TV available then, and trips to the cinema—sadly were only occasional, as my pocket money was very limited.

Thus cycling, reading, walks and talks with friends, particularly about books, were part of the richer aspects of life, in this period. The bike explorations were very important, and it was necessary to escape from time to time from home, which in that period was not the happiest of places, because of the continuing conflicts between my parents about New Zealand versus Wales. Sometimes, when I felt I could afford it, I would go into town, and there in the city centre on Queen Street, was this one special place, the Kardomah Coffee House! Going there seemed very sophisticated, and one could choose the type of coffee you wanted, and perhaps meet a friend, and think that you were really—'living it up!'

By contrast, being at home in this period was not easy, as things were economically depressed, and one felt a little isolated and almost claustrophobic because of the battle between my parents about having left New Zealand. From time to time the situation would be slightly lifted by a visitor from elsewhere. Uncle Harry came on a visit from New Zealand, and he was always very lively and good fun. He had been by himself on a holiday to Italy, and came back raving about the beauty of the Italian women, their extraordinary vivaciousness, their incredible busts, and other features!

I had a love of cinema, but unfortunately could only occasionally afford to go and see a film. I had become a member of the Anglo-Jewish Association, and through that was able to borrow a new film from them, which we could show at school. However, that had some strange repercussions. The film which we showed at Cardiff High School was a film about the creation of a Kibbutz in the desert, and it was called 'House in the Desert'. This was shown to the all-boy audience at school, and had some unexpected reactions. In the early days it showed that the settlement was an all male settlement, busy trying to create agriculture, housing and some sort of life in a harsh desert environment. Then it showed the first woman being brought to join that community, and I shall not forget the dialogue in the film—at that point. The film then stated that not so long after the first woman came to the Kibbutz, the first baby was born, and all the men felt that the baby was theirs! The double-entendre immediately appealed to this all boy audience, and there were great hoots of laughter, which took me some time to live down!

There were some very innovative aspects of life at Cardiff High. Once again I was involved in the school drama society, and I seem to recall we were involved in productions of Julius Caesar, Volpone, and other classics. In addition, there was a school competition relating to hobbies, and this gave me my first chance to produce a large model for an ideal planned town. That was in 1949, and I produced a model for the creation of a new port on the Gulf of Akaba, where Israeli soldiers had just established a camp, on this arm of the Red Sea. It was early days for such a town to be built, but when 20 years later a port and a tourist town was properly created at Eilat, I felt I had beaten the Israelis to it! As a result of winning a school prize with this large model, which was about 4ft long by 3ft wide, the Headmaster encouraged me to think about town planning as a career. My reading was also leading me in that direction, and this idea had enormous appeal. My problem was that I had a love of three subjects at school, namely history, geography and art, and these were my best subjects. In fact, I had the opportunity to go and do history at Cambridge, but with encouragement of the Headmaster—Mr Diamond, and of my father, who had been discouraged from taking his choice of career, I did in fact go ahead with the planning option.

In the late 40's, I felt the doors were starting to open to the future. My reading and explorations about and in planning, were making me seriously think about a career in town planning: my involvement in the Zionist Youth Movement made me think about the possibility of becoming a planner in Israel, and building new towns in the deserts and mountains there, and the fact that a five year planning course was available in Manchester seemed to open the gates for me. Lowdermilk's book on Palestine suggested that planning and Zionism were interdependent concepts!

Three things happened in 1951 that really represented the threshold of life ahead and important explorations. Firstly, in the summer after having worked in slave-like conditions on a market garden near Cardiff, in order to earn some cash, I was able to afford to go on a hitch-hiking trip to France with Bimbo, and that was a great time of exploration all the way across France. Secondly, I was able to make a short visit to the Festival of Britain in London and that was enormously exciting, as I was so keen on landscape design, modern design of furniture and buildings, that this was an enormous encouragement for me. Also, there was the Festival of Wales, which was part of the Festival of Britain, and Cardiff Habonim put on a great display of Israeli folk-dancing, singing, and gymnastics—at the

Maindy Stadium, in which I had a starring role! Finally in that year, with my grandpa's death, I felt that a big family break was occurring, and thus going off to Manchester seemed to be a timely chance for an exciting and independent future.

CHAPTER NINE

Migrants to the USA and Australia

Already it will be seen, from earlier on in the book, that we are a very mobile family. From the family's roots in Poland I have pointed to the links through to the United Kingdom on the one hand, and from there on to California in one direction, and to New Zealand in another direction. At this stage I'd like to introduce links elsewhere, namely to the wider United States on the one hand, and to Australia on the other.

Grandpa Michael's sister Bertha had apparently married someone by the name of Jan Rubini who came from Sweden, and they settled in New York, and became one of the American branches of the family. The Rubini children were talented musicians, giving major public performances in their youth. In turn, their children moved to California, where they had musical careers in the movie industry. My daughter Abby, has maintained contact with them.

Another of Grandpa's brothers, namely Joseph, also settled in London either at the end of the 19th or the beginning of the 20th Century. His son Alfred—married Kitty, and they developed a family in London who were my father's cousins, and of whom he was very fond.

These London Travises were a warm and delightful family. Alf and Kitty had some three children, a daughter Norma, then a daughter Audrey, and finally son called Derek. This was a section of dad's London family whom we met after we returned to Britain in 1946, and were first reconnected with, by attending their Audrey's wedding to another Londoner, by the name of Gabbie Woolfson. Audrey's sister Norma, who had served in the Women's Armed services, had already gone off to the States after her marriage to a GI, and they had settled in Levitt-town on Long Island. Norma's wedding to an American seemed to have started the trend off, because not only had she settled on Long Island, but after Audrey Travis's wedding, they in turn, went off and settled in New York City. They were to be followed, over time by brother Derek Travis, who went to New York where he married a New York girl, and with all their three children settled over there, the parents, Alf and Kitty, also went and joined them in New York.

Some year's ago when our son Theo, married his American wife Madelyn—in the early 1990's, we went to their wedding in New Jersey. Afterwards, we also had the chance to go up to Long Island, and see all the New York Travises,' who were then partly settled in New York itself, and partly up on Long Island. Over time Audrey, who had three children in New York, did eventually move to Denver in Colorado, where one of her married children had moved, leaving her other children behind in New York. She is now retired, and lives within a large retirement community down in Florida. Derek, who married an orthodox Jewish New York wife, rather to our surprise, as Derek had served in the Coldstream Guards in London and seemed rather an establishment character. It was surprising that he made such a choice of wife. His two daughters went on Aliyah and settled in Jerusalem, Israel, and there they both married, settled down, and have brought up families. Sadly, eventually Alf and Kitty died, but Norma and her children remained in New York, some of Audrey's children remained in New York, though Audrey was settled in Florida, and Derek, in his retirement, moved from New York to Jerusalem. We have maintained some contact with these former 'London Travises,' as we think of them, via our daughter—who is friendly with Derek's two married daughters in Jerusalem.

A part of the Travis/Dalley family in Australia (Oz), 1980's?

As far as the Australian links are concerned, the migration of my Uncle Reuben, ie my mother's brother, to Australia in the 1920s—has been mentioned earlier, and as was indicated, we first met him in Melbourne in 1939. At that stage he was married to his first wife, and arising from that marriage they had a son who was born in 1933, called Joseph Lionel. For many years we lost contact with this brother of my mother's, but when we did eventually re-establish contact, he had divorced his first wife, and was now living in Adelaide, where he was married to a second wife. It so happened that in 1976, Philippa and I went to Australia, where I was speaking to a bi-ennial congress of Australian planners, which was taking place in Adelaide, so the opportunity occurred to meet this uncle once again. By that stage Uncle Reuben was somewhat decrepit, and was in a wheelchair, but he lived with his delightful, lively second Australian wife, and her family by an earlier marriage. It was a delight meeting these lively, hearty, extrovert Australians in Adelaide. We eventually learned that Uncle Reuben's son by his first marriage, Lionel, who had eventually become a Jeff Bradley, was settled in Perth in Western Australia, where he was a successful disc jockey!. We found out that sadly Jeff died in 1979, aged 46, in Western Australia, but understand from my cousin Sheila (Uncle Max's daughter), that Jeff was divorced.

However, a further link with Australia had developed because my other cousin Audrey Travis (!!), with whom I'd grown up with in Wellington, New Zealand, had married Bob Dalley—a N.Z. carpenter in Wellington, and later gone to Australia. Bob, who was a very easy going Kiwi, keen on golf and Bridge, had won a contract to build Wharves in Sydney Harbour, and as a result of that, Bob and Audrey and their two children, John and Karen, had settled in Sydney. Because of their move there, that section of the family had now grown up in Sydney, and my Uncle Harry from Wellington had followed them, and had also settled in the suburbs of Sydney. Bob and Audrey did well economically in Australia. Following on from his contracts in Sydney, Bob went into property development in Sydney, and then also found that development opportunities were cropping up in Queensland, where he started developing large-scale marinas. As a result of Bob's ventures in Sydney and in Queensland, Bob and Audrey became property multi-millionaires, and moved from a modest home in Sydney, to an elaborate harbour-side home on Point Piper, one of the plushest locations in Sydney. There they developed an estate with a wonderful home, with gardens flowing down to the harbour side, and moorings there for their boats.

On one of our two visits to the Dalleys in Sydney, we found that life was very luxurious for them, and in turn for their children. John and

Karen, (Bob & Audrey's offspring), have both got married and brought up families in Sydney. John's wife is South African, and Karen's husband is an Australian Mining Engineer, who has moved into 'the big time'. They live this high society life in the great metropolis. For a period my cousin Valerie also moved over from Wellington to Sydney, and lived there, before eventually returning to New Zealand. This time she went to live in Auckland, as her husband had died earlier, so went where her brother Barry had now moved. After Barry had moved to Auckland and got married to a wife from New Plymouth, they brought up the family of two daughters and a son in Auckland. Barry had become a Barrister, and later a Judge in Auckland, so they too had found an affluent life style 'Down Under', but in Auckland—the N.Z. metropolis, and not Sydney.

Thus part of the Travis family had moved from Wellington to Sydney, and when the Dalley's were established in Sydney, Uncle Harry and his second wife Vera had followed them there, and eventually Uncle Joss's widow Lily, moved to Australia, and settled at Surfers Paradise in Queensland. That is the "Miami of Australia", and that is where she retired, and spent her latter days.

Uncle Harry died in Sydney, as also did his lovely daughter Audrey, and when we last heard about Bob, he was at a near-death situation, also in Sydney. However, much to our surprise, the children of John and Karen, whom we thought were so well established in Sydney, have surprised us by settling in Israel, and thus not remained part of this affluent Australian society!! One of John's sons has settled in Tel Aviv, and I think two of Karen's children have also settled in that same city. It seems that now Karen and her husband Gary Zamel, in addition to their homes in Sydney and New York, maintain a third home in an apartment block in central Tel Aviv, and I think John also now has an apartment there too, so that the Australian Dalleys seem to split their time between Sydney, New York, and Tel Aviv, much to my amazement!

It is curious the way things go! Though part of the 'London Travis' are still settled in New York, part of them are in Miami, but another section of them, that is Derek and his two daughters, are now settled in Jerusalem. Of the Australian family, though Karen and her husband and John and his wife—still live part of the time in Sydney, their children are settled in Tel Aviv. Curiously, the Australian section of the family looks as though it is being superseded by their settlement in Israel! Thus today we're an even more scattered family, with part of the family being in Britain, part of the family being in Sydney, Australia, some in New York, others in Auckland, New Zealand, part of the family now being in Tel Aviv, and part of it in Jerusalem. Heaven alone knows where the next generation is going to be! The mobile Travii seem to be upping and moving yet again . . . .

CHAPTER TEN

Manchester Encounters

Arriving at Manchester's soot-encrusted London Road Railway Station, I was suddenly in the "Industrial North of England" in 1951. From the black soot-covered, neo-gothic towers of Dover Street, to the horse-drawn wagons pulling their loads over the wet, cobbled streets of the inner city, this was 'the North'. In 1951 Manchester was still subject to the all obliterating smogs in which not only did the buses and other traffic stop, but the streets of the city seemingly evaporated—as one walked in the choking gloom towards town, holding hands with strangers. They were also seeking their way either to the Free Trade Hall for a Halle Concert, or trying to get to some other destination in the city centre.

Manchester in 1951 was the traditional industrial north, complete with dark satanic mills, grey faces, and the dreary drabness that had been created by a hundred years of industrialism. The kids in Inner City Levenshulme were still being sewn into their underwear for the winter, and groups of beggars still sat outside the pubs, waiting for a free drink or a sixpence, or something else that might raise their spirits. Here in this strange world I arrived to become a student for five years in this wet, dark, unknown city—that was now to be home.

Several things helped me quickly to fit in and find my own little social circle. After registering and joining the Victoria University of Manchester, I quickly joined U.M.A.P.S.—The University of Manchester Architectural and Planning Society—where I soon joined two others, Mike Pearson and Bill Cowburn, to launch a new design magazine called 244. The name of the magazine was based on the number of the building on Oxford Road where the School of Architecture was based, and it was partly here and partly across in Dover Street, that we started our student lives.

The first thing I needed to do was to find "digs"—somewhere to live—and initially this was affected by my parents' decisions. They had asked me to take Jewish digs in North Manchester, which was not very convenient, as the University was in South Manchester, and the Jewish part of North Manchester seemed to be incredibly remote from it. Thus I started for the first few months staying with a family called the 'I.' family, living in Upper Crumpsall, but this was not very satisfactory. They were a pleasant enough family, Zionist in character, but lived according to the current style of the frugal North at that time. This meant that there was a coal fire in the living rooms downstairs, but upstairs in the guest bedroom there was just a small electric heater in the corner, complete with coin-box, in which you had to feed your supply of shillings, to generate some marginal warmth! As the bedroom was where I attempted to study at night, it became necessary to put on an overcoat, gloves, a scarf, and an extra sweater to try and do some work in the bedroom. This was not very acceptable. In addition, the family had an unmarried daughter whom they expected me to take out regularly, and I did not like that part of the tenancy arrangement! Thus very quickly I moved down to Victoria Park, the leafy old suburb not far from the University, where most students either had digs, or were finding places in the limited number of Halls of Residence.

I took digs with the "L" Family, which proved to be an interesting and curious adventure. It seemed that the three students who were staying in that house, were seen as illegal, as Mr L. was a policeman, and the police were not allowed to have students in their homes. Thus we had to swear to secrecy, in order to remain in these digs. The family were pleasant enough, and as the policeman was busy studying law in order to become a solicitor, it was quite surprising when after a relatively short time, they announced he had qualified as a lawyer, and had obtained a job as the Magistrate for Suva, the capital of Fiji in the South Pacific! Hence, once again I was moving house, and this time I moved on to the curious but quaintly-named suburb of Chorlton-cum-Hardy. This was a time of exploration for me in Manchester, so I also explored what was becoming the trendy Didsbury District of South Manchester, which was a colourful place that had living within it the 'Yakipaks'. These were the exotic Spanish-Portuguese immigrants, who had come as part of the carpet trade and textile trade from Baghdad and Aleppo to Manchester, and now formed the Sephardi Jewish Community of South Manchester, as compared to the more conventional East European—or Ashkenasi Jews, who lived in North Manchester.

The Chorlton-cum-Hardy home base became a colourful and important one for me. There I took over the attic of No.6 Maple Avenue, and had permission to paint it, so I made this bed-sit in the attic into 'rainbow roof', and this was to become my home for most of the time that I lived in Manchester. The landlord and landlady, the 'J.' family were a colourful pair. He had been a professional comedian, and she had been an opera singer, and they were full of humour and jokes. They were kind, warm, and welcoming people to see, and to whom to pay the weekly rent. The house had three or four bedsits in it, and the occupiers of the bedsits shared an upstairs kitchen—dining room, and also shared a separate bathroom. When I first came there, there were two other tenants, one a young man who came from Holyhead in North Wales and the other, a strange sinister character, who looked as though he'd come out of a Jack the Ripper story. They were to be followed by a sequence of other tenants who became lively colleagues and friends, living at No. 6 Maple Avenue. The house was close to the main shopping street of Chorlton, and there were all the shops you needed, in order to do self catering.

Not far away, about five minutes walk from the house, was a new small enterprise called The Piccolo Theatre. This became one of the places that I started going to, to see productions there, and became friendly with one of the actors at the theatre, who had come up from Bristol Young Vic and his name was Eric Thompson. Eric later was to gain fame on TV later, when he provided the voices for the very popular show' The Magic Roundabout.' He became even more famous through his actress daughter Emma, who became one of the biggest names both on the stage, and in English cinema. My own interests in the theatre led me early on to join the Manchester University Drama Society, and there I felt very much at home after my experiences of drama groups both in Cardiff on one hand, and in Wellington, New Zealand on the other. Our first big production was of James Elroy Flecker's 'Hassan', where I had a major role both on the production side, and in set- and costume-design. This involved some curious and challenging tasks, such as my having to find three live camels for the stage production, which involved actors travelling on the Golden Road to Samarkand. This required my visiting Bellevue Zoo in Manchester, and persuading the zoo-keepers that for a few nights we could borrow some of their camels, to have them performing on the stage of the University Theatre!! This took a lot of pleading and persuading, and when we did eventually get them there for a try-out, we found it was somewhat of a hazard, because of the frequency that the camels relieved themselves on the stage of the theatre!

The five year planning course at the University was an Honours Degree Course which had only started a year or two earlier, and was still in it's developmental stages. Thus, some key subjects were missing, and we had to lead protests and form delegations to the staff, to get subjects like sociology and landscape design included in the curriculum. We also had to persuade the staff, that the content of some of the subjects was inappropriate. For instance, in agriculture and rural planning, it seemed inappropriate and unnecessary for us to learn how to milk cows, whereas we did need to know all sorts of things about rural activities, and rural land uses.

The group of planning students was a small group and we were dominated by our very large sister department of architecture, where most of the rather arrogant architects treated the planners as people who "weren't good enough to be architects!" Thus I was very keen as the planning representative on the UMAPS Executive, to prove to the architects that we were as good as them, and became very active not only in the development and publication of the 244 magazine, but also in the organisation of our annual "Hot Pot", and other social events.

In time off, there were good places to escape to—from Manchester. If you took a bus ride out from Manchester, either to Edale or to Hayfield, you could—within a few hours, be climbing Kinder Scout, the highest peak in the Peak District, which is a place of rugged rocky mountains and the grandeur of the moors, to escape to from the soot and grime of Manchester. In the Planning and Architecture Departments too I found some kindred spirits, such as Donald Skelley, who was in the year above me in Planning, and whose mother and grandparents welcomed me to their farmhouse home at Heaton Mersey on the edge of Stockport. Don's father had been a captain of a merchant ship that was sunk in the war. There, on the farm, Don and I would sometimes spend evenings talking, listening to gramophone records, or going together to hear the Halle Orchestra, in the Free Trade Hall. On one big occasion I travelled out to a country house in Cheshire, for Donald's 21st birthday party, which was a great event, meeting not only a wide range of his family and relatives, but his attractive girlfriend from North Wales, and a number of familiar colleagues from the University. As Donald had a powerful motorbike, on which I could ride pillion, during various trips out into the country that became a great source of delight as well.

One evening a group of architects and I were invited to an evening soiree at the home of the Manchester Guardian's Art critic, which of course was located in the Didsbury District. In this fine house there were many exotic indoor plants on one hand, and a number of very good original paintings by great British and French artists, on the other hand. At one point this lady critic turned to one of the somewhat embarrassed young architects and said, pointing in a direction that seemed to have nothing other than a very exotic indoor plant, "What do you think of my Sickert?" The flummoxed lad, assuming she was referring to her plant, and not the original painting on the wall, said "It's very impressive, how often do you water it?!' Apart from the very busy life on the course, as we had some 16 subjects to study in the course of the five years, and these ranged from engineering, law, and urban history to urban geography, there were lots of non-academic university activities in which one could get involved.

The author, BBC war correspondent, Manchester Guardian
special correspondent, & researcher—Alexander Werth,
mid-1950's in Manchester, UK.

As already indicated, I became very active in UMAPS and in the University Drama Society. I also was persuaded, after a year or two, to join the University Jewish Society and there I met several ex-Habonim people whom I knew from my camping days, so I soon had a very active student life not only in the department and in the drama group, but also in Jewish student activities as well. I went on to the National Executive of the IUJF, and became the Universities Zionist Officer, in my later years at Manchester. In the Architecture and Planning Departments of the University, most of the students were male, but we had a few lively female students as well, they gave a much more normal feeling to the studios, as well as to social occasions. In our year we had three female colleagues, and one of them—Isobel, who came from Hertfordshire, was both a friend, and a work colleague. She was staying in a Women's Hall of Residence (in those days of segregation!), and it was good to go there for the 'Annual Formal', as her partner, complete with tails!! Not even a dinner suit sufficed then!

In addition to various friends made through these different societies and groups, there were seven people who had a considerable influence upon me during my Manchester period. The first of these was Alexander Werth, a distinguished Russian/French writer who took over one of the adjacent bed-sits in Maple Avenue for a few years, during the time that he was the Senior Simon Research Fellow at Manchester University. Alex was an extraordinary character, whose father had been an engineer in Revolutionary St. Petersburg, and he (Alex) had left Russia in the 1920s or '30s, to go first to Paris, and then to Glasgow, where he did his further degrees, before joining the staff of the Manchester Guardian, for whom he was a correspondent for a number of years.

During the Second World War, Alex was the BBC's main war correspondent in Stalingrad in Russia, during the siege. After the War, he again became a correspondent, before becoming an author of a series of major books on France, Russia, and the United States. He was an extraordinarily lively and interesting man, with whom I enjoyed going for walks. His favourite walk was through Manchester Southern Cemetery, where he would enjoy his own survival, as compared to all those dead. He mused over the vast piles of frozen corpses, which he had seen in Stalingrad, and noted that there was little to differentiate all the naked dead Germans from the dead Russians! We also had late night chats—over cocoa and potent rum, or over burnt toast, which was his speciality! Alex was writing two books, whilst he was in Manchester, and became a source of great stimulus, and encouragement in my student days.

Through Alex, I met the Chapmans—that is Brian Chapman, Professor of Government at Manchester University, and his authoress wife, who were busy at that time writing their seminal book on "The Life and Times of Baron Haussmann". They were lively and interesting companions, whom I got to know well.

Another person whom I met through my tenancy at No. 6 Maple Avenue, was a musician called David Wise. David, originally from Northern Ireland, took over Alex's former bed-sit flat, and was good company, as he was a lively French Horn player in the Halle Orchestra, and each evening after he came back from performances, he would be full of very funny jokes about the exploits of Sir John Barbarolli, who was then the famous conductor of the orchestra. In addition, David also had a Vincent 500 motorbike, so in my student days I would sometimes go motor-biking off on the back of David's bike, and on other occasions go off into the country on the back of Donald's motorbike, which was a Norton 1000. Fortunately, my mother never learned of these great rural rides!

Life was not all fun and joy during my time in Manchester, for though I was on a £200 per term subsistence grant from Cardiff City, it was difficult to manage on this tight budget. The result was at the end of some terms I would run out of money, and tended to have two or three foodless days at the end of each term. On these occasions I would learn how to make (a) the plentiful supply of water, (b) a slice or two of bread, and (c) one tomato or a piece of cheese, sufficient to keep me going for a couple of days. Sometimes on these foodless days, I would avoid lectures, as I didn't have the energy to go to the university nor the money for the bus fare, so would stay in bed, and cope that way. On such days either Olu or Williams would come and help me out. Olu was an architectural student, and friend—in the same year as me, and he was the son of a Nigerian publisher. His splendid full name was Oluwule Olomuyiwa, and he would turn up with a food parcel, which we would share, and relieve the famine that way. On other occasions, one of the off-beat, but good-hearted planning students from Wales, impressively-called Cecil Edward Elgar Williams, would also come—to see if I was alright, complete with a food parcel, to share, and by these means survival was possible!. The friendship with these two truly Christian friends was important, both as part of physical survival on one hand, and for the sense of spiritual support given, on the other. When Olu qualified, and returned home to Lagos, he opened the first successful, all-Nigerian architectural practice, in Nigeria!

The last and perhaps the most important of the influences, was the new Professor who came to head the Planning Department, in the early 1950's. This was Professor Clifford Holliday, who was quite a remarkable character! Cliff Holliday was always to be seen dimly behind a cloud of smoke from his cigarettes, from which he would emerge—complete with his rotund figure, his bow tie and his warm smile, and he lived in a mini world which he took with him. His office was a piece of Palestine, transferred into the soot of Manchester. There in the room were cacti, Alvar Aalto bent-wood furniture, photos of buildings he had designed in Tel Aviv, in Colombo, and Gibraltar. This was all covered by smoke haze, which made you feel that you were in some Middle East market or suq, rather than a miscellaneous office in the University of Manchester. Cliff had been a senior architect, serving the British Mandatory Authority in Palestine, and had worked on the design of churches like St Andrews in Jerusalem, and buildings like those for Barclays Bank in Tel Aviv, and Haifa. He was full of anecdotes, had a lovely quirky sense of humour, and was someone who was ready to share his experiences, his ideas and thoughts with students, as though they were professional colleagues of longstanding. It was under his influence in my third year at Manchester, that in fact I took a job in a new town in Israel, given his encouragement to work in what was still his 'Palestine', and had now become the independent State of Israel. Through Clifford I got to know his family, and it was his son John Holliday, who was to be such a source of support and friendship, when we eventually moved to Birmingham for the first time.

The Manchester student period was important for another meeting as well, because it was during my period as a Manchester student, I think in my fourth year there, that I went to Liverpool to attend a student conference, and at that IUJF conference in Liverpool, met a very special young lady, called Philippa, whom I became keenly interested in, and who—a few years later, was to become my wife.

The long summer vacations during the five year course at Manchester, were important for two reasons, firstly as a time when I could go out and earn some money, to help supplement my very inadequate maintenance budget from Cardiff City, and secondly also to get some professional experience, before the time that I became a fulltime professional in the planning field. The summers of 1951 and 1952 were significant for the long periods I spent as an agricultural labourer, working on a huge market garden at St. Melons, halfway between Cardiff and Newport. Then I had to get up at six in the morning, was collected on a truck at seven in the morning, and before eight o'clock was at work in the fields, with sacks over my back to keep the rain off, much of the time. The farmer who owned this extraordinary place, seemed to have spent a lot of time studying the layout of concentration camps, as in the centre of his farm he had built a watch tower (!!), and he occupied the top platform on this tower, where he had binoculars and a whistle. If he saw anyone who was not doubled up working in the fields, or had spent more than a minute of two in a hedge relieving themselves, he would blow his whistle, to get people back to work. Working with a group of rough lads from inner Cardiff and Newport with their colourful language in which the 'F' word seemed to represent every second word of every sentence, you got a view of life which was very different to that in British Universities in the 1950's.

In 1953 I needed to get some practical experience of Spanish, which was my choice of a foreign language, so as I've explained earlier, I went by sea to Spain, and took a summer university course at Santander, in the North of Spain. In 1954, under Prof Holliday's influence, I took a job through P.A.T.W.A. that is Professional and Technical Workers Aliyah. This job was as a planner to work for the summer in the new town of Ashkelon, for the Afridar Corporation. The employer was a Development Corporation based in South Africa that was funding the renovation of the historic town of El Majdal, and the creation of new neighbourhoods around it, to form a new city for immigrants settling in the country in 1954. The story of that experience is given later in the book.

In 1955, in my last summer vacation before ending the course at the University, I took a job as a planner in Basildon New Town, in Essex, and there did an exciting variety of things. I worked part of the time with the famous landscape architect Sylvia Crowe, working on the landscape master plan for the new town, and upon landscape features like the town park, and other elements within the plan. Sylvia Crowe's seminal books were later to give the British Landscape Profession a new vocabulary of landscape design. I also worked on some design aspects of the new pedestrian city centre, which was being developed during that period. Further information about that time in Basildon crops up later in the book.

In the summer of 1956 I graduated from the Planning course with a First Class Honours Degree in Planning, and that was an exhausting end to that five year study process. I had worked on a thesis on town park design, which involved many long nights of writing, drawing, and typing, and this left me totally exhausted. However, the winning of a First Class Honours Degree opened up a number of opportunities for me, and it seemed that this first degree was going to be a springboard for future developments.

There were at least two choices available to me, first of all to do a Masters Course at the Harvard Design School in Massachusetts in the United States, or secondly I was offered a job as a result of my successful experience in Ashkelon, as the Town Planner for Beersheba, which was an expanding city in the Negev Desert, in the South of Israel. The choice between these two options was however constrained by the difficult economic situation my parents found themselves in, at that stage. They begged me not to go abroad, either to the United States or to Israel, as they desperately needed my financial help at that time, and therefore I thought I would first do my National Service, from which I had had deferment during my period of university studies. However, when I went for my medical, I was turned down as unfit, by the doctors, who said that I had a "dicey heart condition". So, in a state of shock, I went off with friends climbing in North Wales and the Peak District, before deciding what to do. My heart flutters, or palpitations were to crop up again, from time to time, over the years, and not get finally sorted out till I was eighty years old!

Having had work experience in Basildon New Town in the previous summer, I contacted them again, and was immediately invited to take a fulltime job there with the Development Corporation. This would give me an immediate income, from which I could help my parents at that stage. However, I was already very friendly with Philippa, during this period, and was increasingly keen to get married, but this was something which my parents wanted me to delay, in the hope that I could help them financially for a longer period. The wedding was therefore delayed for about a year and a half, whilst I saved for that on the one hand, and was helping my parents financially, on the other. I did feel, however, that my marriage priority was not going to be changed, even by my parents' needs, and after this five year period at Manchester, I looked forward to a new life, with my wife, working, and living together in Basildon.

CHAPTER ELEVEN

Geddes, and practicing Town Planning

Professor Patrick Geddes was an extraordinary Scot who was born in 1854 at Ballater on the Dee, and died in 1932 at Montpellier in France. This impressive man was the greatest inspiration for the town planning movement in Britain, and as a result of his truly remarkable teaching, thinking, and practice around the world, laid the foundations for the best practice and philosophy of the profession of town planning. In a memoir of this sort it would be inappropriate to write a full history about the very wide-ranging and rich contribution of this one man, not only to the evolution of the planning profession in the United Kingdom, but to a worldwide development.

Geddes as a great sociologist, biologist, and planner, was a thinker, a teacher and a practitioner to whom we all owe an enormous debt. He was that rare thing—a great creative thinker, who could synthesise many influences and ideas in his teaching, and then show how they could be used in practice, which ranged from work done in the old town of Edinburgh, to the great park he created at Dunfermline in Scotland, through to the range of professional work which he did later in India on the one hand, and Palestine on the other. His production of the one book 'Cities in Evolution', was supplemented by his lecturing in the UK, France, Germany, United States, India and further afield. His impressive professional practice was done

The great Professor Patrick Geddes—Planner, Sociologist, Biologist, and Planning Consultant in the 1920's

in Edinburgh, Dunfermline 1904, Jerusalem, Tel Aviv 1921/2, Haifa 1930, and at many places throughout India. His planning contribution is far too little known, and far too little recognised. Mairet's book on Geddes, clearly shows the wide range of his professional work.

By accident, I started discovering the writings and work of Patrick Geddes in my teenage explorations at Cardiff Central Library. What dominated most of the planning writing was the very extensive practice and writings of Sir Patrick Abercrombie, who was central to the field of planning consultancy from the 1930's up to the 1950's. However, it is very important to explain the differences between these two approaches. Abercrombie was a great planner in the Haussmann tradition of grand plans, imposed on either virgin landscapes or cities that had been destroyed by earthquakes, aerial blitz, or fires. In contrast, Geddes was not a maker of 'grand plans', but a sensitive re-adjuster of structures in a more biological way. Moreover, Geddes showed an approach that was amazingly innovative. He saw that cities are like people: they are complex, sensitive mechanisms and organisms, that require delicate surgical intervention. He was the first to see that the planner really needs to be a careful urban surgeon, removing the decay and rot from the body of a town or city, just as a surgeon removes cancerous pockets from the human body. This medical analogy is very important indeed, because what one sees in Geddes' thinking, is a synthesis of sociology and biology. He brings together an understanding of history, geography, and the whole nature of movement, life and death within natural and man-made systems. Whilst many architect-planners and engineers have imposed their ideas on cities, carving their routes through like reckless developers, and ignoring urban grain and texture, Geddes saw that one needed to work with existing structures, so that the process of change could be biological or evolutionary, and not revolutionary in its damaging effects upon the living fabric of complex mechanisms, like cities.

What I realised about halfway through my life, was that the education which I had been fortunate enough to experience at Rongotai College at Wellington in New Zealand, had been Geddesian in its philosophy. The understanding of folk, work and place, how people settle in a location, how their activities grow out of the resources at a location, and how physically the form of towns grow out of a set of natural circumstances, which people make the most of, was all understood by Geddes. It was also understood by those who conceived the form of developmental education, which students at Rongotai experienced, and as already indicated—it was Geddesian in nature.

When in the 1950's I went to work during my summer vacation at Basildon New Town, a background in Geddes' reading helped me to understand the strange nature of the existing settlements that were located on the new town site. Our role in shaping a new town, on top of these existing settlements, was a complex one. This knowledge and understanding was even more important when after my graduation from Manchester, I went to work full-time for two crowded years at Basildon New Town, and could bring this earlier background to that situation.

London's East End was historically a reception area for immigrants coming to the big city. Over hundreds of years, Huguenots from France, Irish labourers escaping from potato famines, East European Jews escaping from pogroms, all came to the East End to find work and hope. Eventually successful migrants moved on to the North East and North West of London. By the 1920's some moved out into South Essex—to the east of London.

Stage 1 of Basildon New Town's pedestrian centre, where
the author worked and lived in the later 1950's.

The site chosen for Basildon New Town was a curious one. It
was a stretch of non-descript territory, well to the east of London,
south of the arterial road which connected London to Southend.
There in this stretch of rolling country in the 1920's, unemployed
people from the East End had gone out, some by road, others by
train to the little railway stations at Pitsea and Laindon, and created
scattered villages. The settlements were of low cost shacks in which
they lived for the period of the Great Depression. There people
created subsistence small holdings, and very modest houses, which
were something like improved versions of the shanty towns, or
Favelas, that you find on the edges of cities in South America. The
big first task in the new town was partly to re-house these people
who lived in substandard shanties, and help with the renovation
and improvement of some of the more substantial buildings in
the villages. Some little shopping groups were found in places

like Pitsea, and there was a need to clear away the sub-standard development, so as to develop industrial areas, residential neighbourhoods, and a town centre for some 80,000 people, who would be moved as so-called "urban overspill" from the East End of London, into this new city in South Essex.

I was very fortunate that in my early work with the Development Corporation, in my student days, I had the privilege of working with the great landscape architect Sylvia Crowe. She was devising the Landscape Plan for the whole new city, and this experience was an education in itself. The Landscape Plan tried to take into account two small key hills that had historic churches on them, recognised where the low hills, and the sweep of landscape lent themselves to creating a town park, and provided the natural location for a city centre. The plan identified the extensive flatland areas near the arterial road access, which would be suitable for the development of new industrial areas. The estates officers' had the difficult, complex, and harrowing task of buying out and demolishing low-standard shacks occupied by now elderly people. It was exciting to get involved also in the city centre plan of Basildon, as this was the first of the new towns to design an all-pedestrian centre, and that was certainly new ground in British new town planning.

There was the opportunity in many small ways to introduce Geddesian approaches, both in my work at Basildon, at the micro- as well as at the macro-scale. Working together with the fine Scottish architect John Stewart on the Long Riding housing development, and some other developments, gave opportunities to use innovative ideas that Geddes had noticed as representing the finest of practice in French and German town planning.

When in 1956 I returned to work at Basildon New Town, as a full-time member of the planning staff, there were a number of very interesting challenges. One of these was to redesign a neighbourhood, which had been conceived by Sir Basil Spence. He was a famous architect, and the designer of Coventry Cathedral, and was no easy character to deal with, in a situation of confrontation. Spence had prepared a design for the Kingswood neighbourhood of the new town, in which he had used "point-blocks" and other tall buildings, which we saw as totally inappropriate. This was intended to be an area for young families with children, so low, family housing with gardens was needed! Thus my strange task as a young professional man, was to tell Sir Basil that we were rejecting his design, and that I was to design and to have built an alternative design, which would achieve all the objectives that had been set by the Development Corporation.

I had to adjust the road plan, which had already been prepared for the area by Spence, so that the stock of housing, garages and facilities laid down in the Official Brief, could all be achieved on the site. Furthermore, I wished this area to be laid out according to the Radburn principle, the experiment that had taken place in the 1920's in the United States, but had never been replicated in Britain. This meant that the whole area was designed for pedestrian front access to each house, with a rear vehicular access system to all the houses, giving them access via their garage courts at the rear, and segregating the pedestrian and vehicular traffic. The Radburn experiment was something that Geddes was aware of in his latter days, and had advocated, but had never seen anyone use as a design concept in the UK. I was very pleased to implement and complete this neighbourhood, and after its completion to have the opportunity to monitor the levels of satisfaction found by the tenants who came to live in It. From time to time, over the years, I would return to Kingswood to talk to its residents, to satisfy myself that the layout and these ideas involved had worked well, and provided a reasonable environment for the people who lived in this area, which I had designed.

When I first came to live permanently, so to speak, at Basildon New Town I was happy to take a flat in the Long Riding housing development, which had been designed by my friend John Stewart. There I was to live in a third storey corner flat, in a block of flats, which had basically been taken over by pensioners. Thus I became the youngest tenant in this corner block, where everyone else could have been my grandparents, in terms of their ages.

The late 50's was the heyday for scooters. The impact of the film "Roman Holiday" and the emergence of "mods" and "rockers", meant that one of my colleagues Neville Hawker, had bought a Lambretta scooter, in which I bought a half interest. Thus daily, as we both lived in Long Riding, we would travel to work at the Development Corporation offices on our shared Lambretta. There was a good spirit in the offices in those days, the first chief architect, Noel Tweddle, was later replaced by his deputy Anthony Davies, and the lively team of essentially British architects were compatible work—as well as social-companions.

What was complex was actually being a member of the Development Corporation staff, and living in the new town. The tenants moving to the new town from the East End, tended to have evening parties, in which they smashed up the piles of paving stones, which were left to pave the new streets. They used these to crazy-pave their gardens, with what they saw as a free supply of paving stones! We who worked for the corporation obviously did not take part in these "smashing-up parties", and therefore were somewhat socially ostracised by the new locals, who were very much East Enders in their attitude to public property.

After I married Philippa in 1957, I moved house from the flat on Long Riding to a new three-bedroomed house. The new town had a Street Naming Committee, which tried to give new streets names that they considered appropriate for South Essex, and this had some odd results. The street on which we now lived was called 'Bonnygates', and an adjacent street was called 'Curling Tye'.

I was having a quiet running battle at Basildon with many of the architects, whose ideas were much more akin either to Abercrombie, with his grand plans, or to Le Corbusier, with his concepts of great monumental buildings. The need was to have a sensitive small-scale environment, suitable for families with young children, re-housed old people, and in the city centre, some accommodation for young urban-swingers, who could live right in town. Thus the battle was often a hidden one between Geddesian and Abercrombie approaches.

In 1959 I applied for, and obtained a better post as a planner, this time with the London County Council, and took my new job working in the L.C.C.'s monumental offices at County Hall, on the South Bank in London, facing the Houses of Parliament. For some six weeks I commuted from Basildon to work at the LCC, which was a somewhat traumatic experience, and made me vow that I would never again become a commuter. The new job, was very different to my previous post at Basildon. Here I was employed in the North East Group of the Planning Division of the Architect's Department at the LCC, and our task included the last phase in the comprehensive post-war redevelopment of the Stepney-Poplar area of the East End, the rebuilding of the City of London, and the restructuring of some of the North East suburbs of London. Basildon and London were linked as parts of the regional approach to planning developed during World War 11. Abercrombie's County of London Plan, and the Greater London Plan together gave a regional strategy both for new development and reconstruction, with a containing metropolitan green belt, and a ring of 'New Towns' beyond that—to accept London overspill of population. Basildon was one of this set of New Towns.

The Head of North East Group was Percy Johnson-Marshall, an eminent architect/planner, who had had major roles in the reconstruction of Coventry after the blitz, and was later to take the Chair of Planning at Edinburgh University. He had several distinguished deputies working under him, who included and were similar in stature to Walter Bor, a great planner who had come from Czechoslovakia to Britain, and Bruno Schlaffenburg, from Poland. This department was an internationally renowned and important one, and for the first time I found myself working in an environment, where most of my colleagues had come from overseas, in order to get the experience of working at the LCC in London. Thus though my immediate work colleague was Michael Dower, who was British, my other colleagues included Chris Buczynski, originally from Poland; Rom Dylewski, who was temporally visiting from Poland; Renee Martinez-Le Moin who was from Chile, Ian Morison from Western Australia; and Eleanor Smith from the USA. Above us in rank were Tom Bigwood, and Ann MacEwen, who were British! This was the most stimulating group of people with whom to work, and I not only worked with them, but at lunch breaks, would go and play tennis with them on the South Bank, and in the evenings—we would sometimes also socialise.

One of my first tasks was a study of public open space deficiencies in North East London, working with Michael Dower The measure of open-space needs was done on the basis of Abercrombie's County of London Plan, and therefore we were trying to see how much public open space was lacking in this part of London, and how such open space could be provided. This all quickly made me realise how differently Abercrombie's planning was from that of Geddes, as we were supposedly implementing a great new park, which Abercrombie had proposed for the East End, and which was to be called Haggerstone Park. The problem was that though the East End was blitzed in the war, many parts of this proposed park, still had on them multi-storey old factories, slum dwellings, and all sorts of other land uses, which were not public open space! All these existing buildings, were called "non-conforming uses", and the LCC had to buy them out, in order to demolish them, compensate their owners, and then create the open space. On the County Surveyor's estimates, the acquisition of all the existing buildings needed to create this new public open space, would have cost £32.5million! However, the allocation for the whole of London for buying out "non-conforming land uses" was half a million pounds per annum. It seemed I was going to have to live for a few hundred years, in order to achieve this grand Abercrombie proposal!

The range of work that I had to do in London, very much challenged my Geddesian principles. For instance, part of the time I was working on a two-tier planning system, whereby we at the LCC, had to judge and evaluate planning applications, which had been submitted to or by the Metropolitan Borough Councils. One of my tasks was to redesign layouts for housing schemes which came from Shoreditch Metropolitan Borough, which were not acceptable in terms of LCC design standards. I found myself redesigning housing schemes, so as to create some pockets of open space, some public and some private, within Shoreditch. So, we in the upper tier authority tried to achieve better design standards through evaluating and changing the designs of the lower tier authority. Other work was linking with the City of London, on such schemes as the later implementation of the St Paul's Precinct, and the complex Barbican developments. Links had to be created between the high level pedestrian system being created along Route 11 in the City, and new multi-storey housing developments, which had access from first-storey, pedestrian decks.

It was not until my second year at the London County Council, that I had the opportunity to implement Geddesian ideas, when I worked on the Bethnal Green Comprehensive Development Area, with my colleague Rom Dylewski. At that time the Institute of Community Studies was functioning in Bethnal Green, and I took the opportunity to go and meet the staff of that Institute, and through them create informal contact with Bethnal Green residents. In those days, LCC designs were done without contact with the people for whom the schemes were to house! In this new way, I got to know both staff of the Institute of Community Studies, and residents' groups in Bethnal Green, who became unofficial and informal collaborators, as we had no authority to do public participation in those days, but it was something in which we believed. Michael Young and Peter Willmott of the Institute of Community Studies, had published "Family & Kinship in the East End," which had shown the social importance of kinship structures, and the severe disruption caused by slum clearance, and the radical rehousing policies, which placed families inappropriately in new tower blocks.

Bethnal Green was a very interesting area to work in, because it contained historic developments, such as the Boundary Estate. This Estate had been the first redevelopment scheme, carried out in London in the late 19th Century! It had replaced "The Nichol", which was a famous or infamous slum, on which the criminal life of the East End had largely centred. Tragically what happened was that as none of the people from the old slum were re-housed on the new Estate: thus the new model housing in excellent blocks of flats, brought in a new population to the area, whilst the old residents scattered, creating new slums near the sparkling new Estate. Thus we tried very hard in our model Comprehensive Development Area, to use a Geddesian approach to enable local people to improve their own lives while continuing to live in the same place. To this end we worked with staff at Shoreditch Borough Council, and at the Institute of Community Studies, and we had much unofficial contact with local residents groups, so that we could plan with them, and not for,(or often against!) them.

A bonus from this work at the LCC, was the contact with these high calibre colleagues from so many countries, and the links through them to others across the world. Exchange trips were made to Coventry and to Rotterdam, which were both stimulating and educational. Through the friendship with Rom Dylewski, my wife and I were to visit Poland in 1962, and develop what became a long-life working link with Poland. Through Rene Martinez, we developed links with Chile, whilst the friendship with Ian Morison led to our joint working, and later other involvements in Australia. The friendship with Chris Buczynski was to be continued again later, when we worked together in Edinburgh, and our friendship with him, continued until his death in 2012. Thus the many links to people at the LCC, became extraordinarily important and formative, in a long term perspective.

The Geddesian approach to work was not only possible but inherent, in the next stage of my career, when I went to work in Newcastle Upon Tyne. This was in 1962, when I was appointed as one of the core team of the new City Planning Department. This was a small team, assembled by the new city planner, Wilfred Burns, to work under the direction of Councillor Dan Smith. The new Department had to tackle the many economic, physical and social problems of Tyneside, in the 60's. Wilf Burns was an engineer who had worked in Coventry, and was not only a creative person, but was adaptive and sensitive, as well as being radical in his city-wide approach to Newcastle. He was later to become the Chief Planner for England, at the Planning Ministry, setting new standards for practice nationally with his Planning Advisory Group (PAG) Report.

My work at Newcastle, as Director of Research, was to develop a team which could do all the research work for the Review of the Development Plan, plus a wide range of special tasks, such as the examination of the choice of sites for a regional airport, social policy research on deprivation, crime, and prostitution, promotional work on inward capital investment, special studies linked to urban motorway development, pedestrianisation, regional arts development, and a programme of talks to primary schools throughout the city-introducing schoolchildren to the concepts of planning and future social choice. It was an enormous work programme for a two year period, and every 6 months we had to await new personal contracts from the City Council, which was not yet convinced of the value of planning.

Whilst planners like Abercrombie, using their sort of approach, could work effectively upon the layout of new capital cities—like Canberra or Chandigarh, they were not necessarily the right sort of people for re-planning cities that were partly blitzed in war conditions. Totally blitzed centres like Coventry and Rotterdam, may have needed radical approaches, but cities like Newcastle Upon Tyne, needed sensitive planner managers, not radical imposers of plans. I had seen working in London, that the Abercrombie approach—certainly as applied to the East End and the City of London, did not work well. This was because with only partial destruction in those instances, imposing radical new structures did not work, as there were inadequate budgets available, to buy out the so-called "non-conforming users". In his day Abercrombie represented sound mainstream practice, but for a declining society. When growth-needs came, his regional ideas with their containment of metropolitan areas, led to inflation of urban land values, and many new problems, which are still with us today.

Our world's debt to Patrick Geddes is enormous. He was the planner, sociologist, biologist and teacher, who really showed us how in the modern world to carry out sensitive change, that was evolutionary within cities. It was fortunate for me that my belief in Geddes was shared by Professor Sir Robert Grieve, the leading Scot's planner who assessed the candidates to occupy the Headship of the Edinburgh Planning School in the late 60's: this led to my appointment there. Edinburgh had been the home and workplace of Geddes, where he developed the Outlook Tower in the Royal Mile, and carried out his renovation of the old apartment blocks in the Royal Mile, it was one of the great fulfilments of my life, that I was to spend some 8 years teaching planning in Geddes's own Edinburgh. Later, when my work led me from town planning into tourism planning, it was this knowledge of the Geddesian approach, that was again invaluable and vital in the development of a new field of professional activity. The research and doctoral tutoring which I started in Edinburgh, was to be greatly expanded when I took over the Directorship of the large Centre for Urban & Regional Studies, at the University of Birmingham. The 1960's was, however, a special period in Scots Higher Education, when with argued cases you could get public finance to expand a department from 2 or 3 staff, to 16 teaching staff, 4 support staff and 4 secretarial staff, get a move approved to a temporary building, and even get over £300,000 funding for a new purpose-designed, teaching building!

CHAPTER TWELVE

Choosing alternative utopias (including the Satin Shade)

As shown already, in the story of Morris in Chapter 2, and in part of Essie's Story in Chapter 4, there has been a choice in the family's history between two alternative utopias. Dad and the Travis family were attracted to New Zealand and Australia, whilst in my mother's family, (particularly via Max and her grandfather), the pull was to Palestine, and subsequently to Israel. I have already described how the pull to New Zealand, eventually attracted my father and two of my uncles and their families, plus my grandpa. Thus the Travis family was split between Australia and New Zealand, with some outliers in the UK and USA. My maternal great grandpa, actually died in Petach Tikva, in Palestine, where Uncle Max also settled. My Uncle David lived in Israel for a time, and some other relatives on both sides of the family also settled there. Thus there has been a seemingly conflicting pull between these two utopias—New Zealand or Australia, as a promised land "Down Under", and the Zionist dream of going to the Holy Land of Palestine, which later became the State of Israel, in 1948.

From my secondary school days onwards, I saw my potential future as a planner in Israel, but it was not until 1954, that I succeeded in going there. Then I tested-out, in some months of working at Ashkelon, the viability of Israel—as a home and working destination. My brother Con, had also been in 1953, to visit Israel, when as a sportsman, he took part in the World Maccabiah, which took place there. Finally in 1956, I did have the option for permanent settlement in Israel, with the offer of a job, to become the Town Planner for Beersheba.

There have been other Seligman and Tavrogis connections to Israel, because my mother's grandfather finally settled at Petach Tikva, where he died. My father's uncle—known as Uncle Yankel—went to settle in Tel Aviv, and died there in the 1950s, and Derek Travis's daughters from New York, settled in Jerusalem, where they are now bringing up families.

With regard to Australasian connections, the story has already been told of my mother's brother, Uncle Reuben, who first settled in Melbourne, and eventually moved to Adelaide, where he died. Audrey Travis, from New Zealand, who became Audrey Dalley, settled with her husband and children in Sydney, where she died. However, Audrey's children, Karen and John, now spend part of their time in Australia, and part of their time in Israel, because their children have now settled in Tel Aviv!

My cousin Valerie Travis, who was raised in Wellington, New Zealand, subsequently had a period of living in Sydney, but finally settled in Auckland in New Zealand, where she still lives. It is in Auckland, New Zealand, too, where my cousin Barry Travis from Wellington, has finally settled, and brought up his family. Aunty Lily Travis, originally from Wellington, passed her latter days at Surfers Paradise, which is a Miami—like retirement resort, in Queensland, Australia, and my cousin Valerie's daughter, Samantha, also lives in Australia. Valerie Travis (who became Valerie Bermel) has a son who is now married to an American wife, and has his own family. He lives in Providence, Rhode Island, in the United States, having married in Israel, and settled down in the United States!

However, what is confusing is that these two separate utopias, chosen by different sections of the family, seem now to be overlapping, as a result of the actions of subsequent generations. What is significant in terms of World Jewry, is that now nearly half the Jews in the world live in the United States and Canada, whilst the other half live in Israel. Thus very reduced numbers are left in other countries. The total Jewish population in the United States however is steadily dropping, whereas that in Israel is continually growing, and it is likely soon that the majority of the World's Jews may live in the State of Israel, as the Jewish Diaspora steadily declines in numbers. The number of Jews living in both New Zealand and Australia is fairly stable in number. However, as far as the wider Travis/Seligman families are concerned, more will be settled in Israel than elsewhere, though the second largest number may well be in Australia and New Zealand, with a small section left in the UK.

I would now like to turn to my experience of visiting and working in the State of Israel in 1954, when the country was only six years old, since its independence. This was a test period for me, in terms of my views of and attitudes towards Israel, and also a time when many other aspects of life and values became resolved as well. I think of that period of the summer of 1954 as the time of "The Satin Shade"—because of an event, that took place during that visit.

I met Miriam Hellerman on board the S.S. Jerusalem, sailing from Marseilles to Haifa. She was an art student in Paris, going home to visit her family in Tel Aviv, for the summer vacation. During the course of the time that I was working at Ashkelon, she would occasionally come down to see me there, and she invited me to come and visit her family in North Tel Aviv. The family were a middle class family from Germany, who had settled in Palestine in the later 1930's.

Their attractive apartment interior, could have been lifted straight out of Berlin in 1936, and was a model of everything that Bauhaus architecture had represented. The sleek modern furniture, the bentwood chairs, the bold black and white, and natural wood designs,

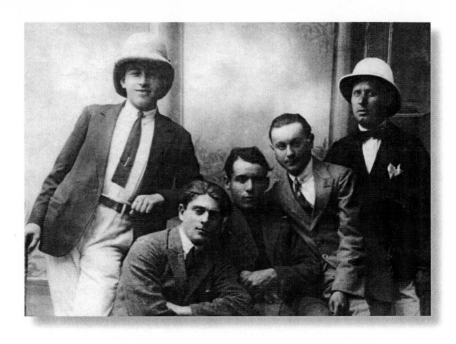

Uncle Max (Seligman), seen on the far left, with colleagues in British Mandatory Palestine, in 1923.

could have been a page out of a 1930's architecture magazine. As I was sitting there, talking to Miriam's doctor father, my eyes focused upon an elaborate standard lamp, with a lampshade made of satin, and as I looked at this, her father spoke. "That satin lampshade is very symbolic" he said. "It represents what you achieve when you're successful in the professions or in business, as opposed to being one of these egalitarian peasants who work in the communal settlements." This symbolic statement that he made, is something that stayed with me throughout the summer of 1954, as I was constantly thinking about the two societies in Israel. I came to the opposite view of the doctor, as I found that the idealistic people who were living simply and sharing things on the Kibbutzim, were impressive and inspiring, but this other side of Israel, of the businessmen and the competitive urban professionals, is one that I found the most unattractive in that society.

That summer in Israel was an extraordinary one for me. It had been generated by the suggestion made by Prof. Holliday of my need to get some modern professional experience, and the fact that Israel, with its many new towns, would be a good place to get it. The journeys to and from Israel were complex—going out by train and ferry to France, and then crossing by train to Marseilles, and boarding an old steamer, the S.S. Jerusalem, which took us, in five days, from Marseilles via Naples to Haifa. The journey back, on the S.S. Artza, was even more colourful. On board were a group of young "Brits", who had spent the summer in Israel, plus a large group of French-speaking Jewish Moroccans. The English group on board included Arthur Rosenberg, Marion Goldwater, and Judy Jacobs, from London—three lively, intelligent and charming travel companions, with whom I had many a good laugh, on board the ship. In addition there were two young English farmers, who had been on farming exchanges to Israel, and one of them, Tom Aynsley, is someone with whom I had long conversations on board. Tom came from many generations of Northumbrian sheep and cattle farmers, and I agreed that sometime after returning home, I would go up to visit him on his farm in Northumberland. This is something that I not only did late in 1954, but it became the basis of a friendship that was to last for over 50 years. In the French-speaking group on board, was a girl from the town of Safi in Morocco, whose name was Reine, (who in England we would call "Queenie"), and she was to become a girl-friend, who later visited me in Manchester.

My impressions of the young State of Israel in 1954 were very complex, and mixed. The Port of Haifa was a delightful Port city and gateway into the country. It is a beautiful city which spreads from the top of Mount Carmel via various levels, down to the waterfront, and is full of trees, fine buildings, and marvellous panoramic views. It seems a very normal Port city, with its industries, its shopping centres, its well-managed Local Authority, and it's feeling of being rather a German, middle-class city, that has been transposed to the shores of the Mediterranean.

Ashkelon, where I was working for the summer, was a very different kettle of fish. The historic town of El Majdal had functioned for hundreds of years, as a small provincial Arab town, dominated by its large Mosque, and with much of the fabric of the town, narrow pedestrian ways leading to courtyard buildings, mainly single storey, and often with Palms in them. The thousands of Jewish immigrants who had poured into the country, were now occupying the buildings of this town, renamed Migdal Ashkelon. Its former Arab residents had fled during the War of Independence. Many of these Jewish immigrants were people who had come from the concentration camps and death camps in Europe, and mostly wanted to find a new life, ideally in Australia, Canada, or the United States. They had reluctantly come to Israel, as one of the few places that would accept them. They were a very motley crew, whom I spent many hours interviewing, and trying to sort out their housing needs, in the new neighbourhoods, that we were building around the old town.

One of the large new neighbourhoods, built in a South African style, was Afridar, where I was staying with two immigrant families from Liverpool. The consultants were South African architects and planners, and the feeling of this neighbourhood was different to elsewhere in Ashkelon, as it included many "Anglo-Saxon" settlers. In Israel, "Anglo-Saxon" means—settlers who have come from English-speaking countries, and thus many of them were from England, the United States, Canada, and South Africa. There were many keen cricketers, and dog-lovers here, and in a curious way the

Afridar neighbourhood, seemed like an English outpost dropped into the Middle East!

The immigrants in the old town, were mainly Europeans who had suffered appallingly during the Nazi period in Europe, but also included quite a number of Moroccan newcomers, as now large numbers of Moroccan Jews, and Jews from other Arab countries, were being forced out of their historic homes where their antecedents had lived for 2000 years, and were now settling in the State of Israel.

Social attitudes in Israel in 1954 were very varied and confusing. When I went to stay on a Kibbutz or a Moshav, I found the people there warm, friendly, welcoming, idealistic and everything that you would expect to find in a utopian society. However, the townees were very different! On some occasions, when there was a long wait for a bus to go from Ashkelon to Tel Aviv, I would attempt to hitchhike. On one occasion a businessman stopped his car, and gave me a lift up to town. Having previously spent quite a lot of time at weekends on the communal settlements, I addressed him as 'friend' or 'Chaver'. The man got very angry, and said, ""you will address me as 'Adoni' or 'Sir'." Obviously he assumed that as a successful businessman, he merited respect from others. It was the sort of response that stayed with me, and made me feel that if one was living in this society, one really needed to live in the idealistic or utopian communities, rather than the cities, which had far too much of the worst, rather than the best characteristics of other cities. Exceptions were Haifa, which was an incredibly normal, socially mixed, and an attractive place, and Jerusalem—which is a city that is quite different to any other in the world. Tel Aviv is hectic, vital, chaotic, noisy, and hedonistic. It is not my sort of place!

Many of these vivid impressions kept making me think again of 'The Satin Shade' in that apartment in Tel Aviv, and what I thought of as the two Israel's—the idealistic on one hand, and the aggressive, capitalistic cities, on the other hand. One weekend I visited my

Uncle Max, who was an extremely successful lawyer, living in a large apartment on Rothschild Boulevard, in central Tel Aviv. He took me out by Shirut (or shared taxi), to the Sharon Hotel in Herzlia. This is a large, comfortable seaside hotel, in a very "up-market" resort, about 10 or 15 miles north of Tel Aviv. There we dined quietly, whilst a small orchestra played, and one had a taste of the good life, for those who were successful in the urban activities of that country. I explained to my Uncle Max, that I was thinking of returning to settle in the country, when I finished my five year degree. He told me not to be a fool, and that the place of the future was Canada, and that I should settle in Canada, and not in Israel. This was somewhat surprising, from someone who had already lived in Israel or Palestine for over 30 years!

One weekend, through a mutual friend, I went to stay on the religious Kibbutz of Sa'ad. This was a young and still fairly raw Kibbutz, near Gaza, on the coast. At that time Fedayin, or infiltrators, were occasionally coming up from the Gaza Strip, and attacking settlements, or visiting places like El Majdal, where perhaps they had lived before, and were trying to retrieve some of their belongings. These evil sounding "infiltrators", were sometimes poor, harmless Arab refugees, just trying to visit their old homes again, and find a few family belongings, like for instance their photo albums, to take back to the refugee camps, in Gaza. What was extraordinary that weekend, and totally unexpected for me, was that there was an Israeli raid upon Gaza, whilst I was staying in that Kibbutz, and during the night, groups of settlers would put on their army gear and become soldiers, take part in this raid, which was complex and hard for me to understand, and to accept at that time. In fact, in the course of 1954, I did not become very hopeful of the idea of peace being achieved between this new Jewish State and the surrounding Arab States. Now all these years afterwards, I feel less hopeful than ever on that being achieved, as the "Arab Spring" and Islamisation—widens the gap between the Israelis and their Arab neighbours.

It's strange to compare the Israel of 1954, with the country today. Then it was a little new country of about 2 million people, settled in a hostile world. Life there then was one of austerity and hardship, there was little in the way of private car ownership. Most people had to queue to get on the crowded buses, and life was harsh, and demanding. Today Israel is a country of about 8 million people. It is a highly developed, and relatively prosperous State, that is enjoying an economic boom. It is now both a developed and sophisticated society. However, despite all these positive things, it becomes more and more remote from its adjacent Arab neighbours. Even though it is technically at peace with Jordan and with Egypt, it is a cold peace, with each of those countries.

When a few years ago I went to visit a former student, who is a friend, and is a Jordanian national, I talked to him in Petra, which is his home town in Jordan. I asked him if I were to have invited him to an event across the border in Eilat, whether he would have come to it. He looked thoughtful for a few minutes, and then said . . . 'I'm not sure . . . I would certainly think about coming for your sake, but I would have to think about the implications.' I said 'What are the implications?'. He said 'The implications would simply be that I would be socially and professionally ostracised by my friends in Jordan, for having gone on a visit to Israel.' Thus one can see how even when intelligent and educated people, who have relatively open minds think this way, how difficult it is to get a real peace between these two countries.

Today of about 8 million population, Israel has 6 million Jews, and 2 million other citizens who are either Muslim, Christian or Druse. However, linguistically it is an extraordinary country. Most people are at least bi-lingual. Virtually the whole population does now speak Hebrew as its first language, but about a million of the population are relatively recently immigrants from the former Soviet Union, and have Russian as their second or first language. Many have French as their second language, as they came as enforced immigrants from Arab countries, which had been under French Colonial rule. Much of the country's population understands and can speak English, so as a tourist or as a visitor, there is no problem travelling round the country if you are an English-speaker.

The future remains very unclear for Israel. There is a high probability of open war between Iran and Israel, as Iran is constantly threatening the annihilation of the new State. If Israel makes a pre-emptive attack upon the nuclear facilities in Iran, heaven alone knows what will happen, as this could lead to one of the biggest conflagrations the Middle East has ever seen. The future is not clear, and is not hopeful, as far as Israel's concerned. However, the vitality of the current existing State there is extraordinary. It is one of the most literate States in the world, with an extraordinary rich academic, musical, cinematic, and theatrical life, and with very high living standards for middle class and higher income families. It is a very heavily taxed country, because of the amount that has to be spent on defence, and the majority of young men have to go for two years for National Conscription, because of the defence system.

I'm glad that I experienced Israel in its early days in 1954, when it was struggling, in a period of austerity, to try and create a new and fair country, under a Labour government. Today under right wing coalition governments, it seems to be heading in inappropriate directions. I can only hope that its future is one of peace, and that its Government and people learn to live with, understand, and find forms of reconciliation and compromise, with the Palestinians, and with Israel's Arab neighbours.

CHAPTER THIRTEEN

Meeting Nigerians and West Europeans

What has been particularly enriching, not only in my student days and subsequent career in practice, but particularly in my teaching days—both in the UK and abroad, has been the meetings with so many lively, and interesting individuals. Whilst these people have been of many nationalities, it is of particular interest to me, that three of those who stand out in my memory, are Nigerians. The first of these, Olu, whom I met in my student days at Manchester, has already been referred to, earlier in the text. Oluwule was interesting both as a friend, and as a work colleague. For his final architectural thesis at Manchester, he worked on the development and design of an Adult Education Centre, for Lagos in Nigeria. We had many long discussions about his design, and about the theories of adult education. One of the areas in which I was able to actively help him, and compensate him for his past kindness in sharing of food parcels with me, was specialist aspects of the design. He wanted there to be a series of partially shaded courtyards within the education complex, and wished to give each of them—a different identity. The way that he decided to do this for each of these spaces, was for each of them to have either characteristic murals, or sculpture groups. This was an area where he was not completely at home, in design terms. My role therefore came to be the design of a number of sculpture groups, finding a way that bridged the approach to traditional sculpting of people in Nigeria, and modern sculpting design by great artists of the calibre of Moore. Some of these groups were designed as adult groups, others were sculptures of family groupings. All of these were distinct and different, so as to help to give a different identity to each of the courtyards. The nature of the murals tried to find a compromise between traditional Nigerian, and modern Europeans designs, and I think they worked well. In these ways I was able to help Olu. When he returned to Nigeria and started his architectural practice there, we corresponded at some length. However, over the years the correspondence became occasional, and rarer. I know that Olu retired some years ago, and I do not know if he is still alive or not. He was a very unusual Nigerian, quiet, non-demonstrative, deeply thoughtful, and creative. He was a person who was a loyal friend, a good correspondent, and a man of integrity. His professional and economic success with his large practice in Lagos, is a tribute to him, this is because he was an honest and strong personality, who was not likely to be corrupted—even in a very corrupt system like that of Nigerian society. The fact that he not only survived, but succeeded magnificently in a very difficult, complex, and corrupt society, like that of Lagos, is an enormous tribute to him.

The second Nigerian with whom I had a lot of contact was a young trainee who was living in London, and was working with me at the LCC in my period there around the beginning of the 1960's. Sadly, as it is so long ago, this is one of the instances where I do not remember his name, though I could still sketch his face, and describe his character. He was very different to Olu. He was a very warm, effusive, lively young man, with an eye for the girls, and someone who very early on—married. The wedding, which took place in North Kensington, lasted some three or four days. Though he was a Yoruba speaking man, from the South of Nigeria, the wedding party still tended to segregate guests, with men in one room and women in another. The food took a lot of adjusting to, for a European. The Cassava root, half-cooked meat, and other so-called "delicacies", were not easy to eat, but the totally Nigerian parties were lively, friendly and warm. In due course, one day when he came to work there was news of the birth of a daughter, called Adetola. I was given the honour of becoming Adetola's Godfather, and thus had to carefully remember her birthdays and other special occasions to celebrate, and send her appropriate gifts. After a few years my young Nigerian colleague moved away, and I also moved. We lost each other's addresses, and sadly over time therefore lost contact, so I don't know what happened to him, and would still very much like to find out.

The third of the Nigerians, Mubo, or Andrew, also came from the South of Nigeria. He came from a typical extended family, where everyone helped each other out socially and economically. It was obviously with the shared backing of the family, that he was able to come and do his Masters Degree at C.U.R.S. at Birmingham University. It was about six months after he had started working on his Masters, that in the course of conversation one day I discovered (a) that he was married, which he had carefully not mentioned before, (b) that he had children, and that his wife and children were with him in Birmingham! Mubo was and is a lovely human being. He is warm, lively, humorous, intelligent, and an extremely loyal character. He took a lot of guiding and help to overcome stylistic problems in research, and had various cultural problems, but did over time get his Masters Degree, and I had great pleasure in seeing him graduate at the University.

After this he decided to go on for his Doctorate, and wanted to do a major work about the approach to tourism planning in Nigeria. This was no small order. For I think two years or more, I worked very closely with Mubo on his demanding and important Doctorate, but it became clear over time that he was having financial problems, and was choosing between paying fees, and getting food for his family. Ultimately we solved this, by my paying his fees, and the family in Nigeria sending over more cash to help his family at least have adequate food. Thus he was able to finish off his thesis, and to graduate with his Doctorate from the university. After this he returned to Nigeria, hoping to enter the tourism profession there, but problems arose. The big problem was that no-one else in the tourist industry in Nigeria had a Doctorate, and people did not want to employ someone who was more qualified than themselves! He therefore had to go back for a period and stay with his wider family, and draw upon the financial help of the extended family, to survive for a period that must have been something like a year or year and a half. There was then a reorganisation of the States of Nigeria, and a new State was added to the Federal Nation, and there he managed to get a job as the Tourism Director for the new additional State that was created. I'm happy to say I still have occasional contact with Mubo, who is successfully holding down that job till this day, and from all evidence, is doing very well in the complex Nigerian political situation. Mention of Mubo's doctorate, reminds me of the fulfilling tutoring work I did on so many doctoral theses in Birmingham. This related to the outstanding quality of work done by Jim Armstrong, John Towner, Zbig Karpowicz, and Fouli Papageorgiou.

My visits to West European countries over the last 50 years, have been many in number, and for different reasons. Firstly, there have been visits to various countries to take British students on study tours, to examine and compare the way that other planning systems function. Secondly, there have been contracts to do consultancy work in various European countries. Thirdly, and increasingly over the years, I have been asked to go and give lecture series in various European countries, and occasionally examine either courses, or help in the vivas of Doctoral students. Tutoring to Ton van Egmond in the Netherlands, to Zak Kaikis from Greece, Marko Koscak from Slovenia, and Ian Jenkins-who was in Wales, and is now teaching in Switzerland, has all been a source of fulfilment. These West European visits have covered much ground, and included the countries of Denmark, Holland, Belgium, Norway, Sweden, Germany, France, Italy, Luxembourg and Spain. In fact it is hard to think of any European countries in West or Eastern Europe that I have not had the official opportunity to visit, over the last 50 years. Most interesting of all has been the rich variety of individuals whom I have met. In so many cases, they have reflected the character, quality, and cultural values of the countries in which they live. As almost all of the individuals about whom I wish to write are still alive, I'll refer to them by their first names only, so that I'm free to talk about them fully and openly.

The first of the countries to which I'd like to refer is Denmark, as early on in my teaching career I found it useful to take British student groups to Greater Copenhagen to see the planning work which was being done on the Greater Copenhagen Plan on the one hand, and on Danish National Plans, on the other. This involved several visits to, and stays in, Copenhagen and its region, as well as visiting other places, around the country. Two important early contacts were the Professor of Planning in Copenhagen, and the Deputy Head of the National Planning office. The first of these was a delightful man with a great sense of humour, and the second was a very talented, thoughtful, and lively woman who had reached almost the top of the profession in that country. Through these two people I met Bent Juel who had become the Head National Planner in Copenhagen and was a key liaison person as well, on the Greater Copenhagen Plan.

Bent was a married man with two children, who lived in the suburbs of Copenhagen, and early on he invited me back to his beautiful courtyard house, to meet the family, and have the chance to relax there one weekend. Over time I got to know Bent Juel, his wife, son and daughter, very well, and in many ways he taught me much about Danish characteristics. He did not originally come from Copenhagen, but was from a farming family that lived near Odense, the second city of Denmark. He is someone who speaks very quietly and slowly, he's very thoughtful, and has a gentle sense of humour, rooted in the countryside, to which he feels a great attachment. The native residents of Copenhagen are hearty extroverts, but Bent was very much in contrast to the locals, and gave one the flavour of a timeless and abiding countryside, which exists beyond the big city.

One year Bent and his wife Lissie suggested we exchange houses for a holiday, and that seemed a great idea. However, when we arrived in Copenhagen, complete with our three children, they were there—waiting for us in the house, to show us where everything was and how everything worked. After a day or two together, we were all getting on so well that they decided that they would stay and holiday with us, rather than going off to our house. Through them we got to know the suburbs, as well as the city of Copenhagen, and with all the children, got to know the delights of the playgrounds and facilities at the Tivoli Gardens, in particular! At one point Bent said that perhaps we should go to stay on their farm for a while, and we discovered that the family owned a farmhouse and small farm, on the island of Langeland. Langeland was a delight. The peace and quiet of that flat island, with its fields full of rich wild flowers, and country inns, or kro's, all added to this becoming a deeply memorable and special time with a very kind and generous family of Danish friends. Bent and his family shared with us a love of modern design, and

A 1980 Travis family photo, with the young Sandy (Alexander).(far left), then Abby, Tony, Philippa and Theo—all hosts to many overseas guests.

thus we fell in love with some of the things in their house, like their modern light fittings. Needless to say when they did eventually come to visit us in the UK, they brought for us an exact copy of the light fitting from their living room, which they knew we had liked so much.

Later Bent left Copenhagen to become the City Architect and Planner of Aarhus, a large city on the coast of Jutland. Now he has retired and still lives there, but we do keep in occasional touch. Through him I have learnt to know and love Denmark, the character of its people, the loyalty and trustworthiness of Danes. A characteristic story about the Danes, is of how—when the Nazis were going to remove and exterminate the Danish Jews, the Danes overnight took the 7-8,000 Danish Jews by fishing boats to Sweden, so that they would be able to continue their lives safely, there. This shows how the Danish people are brave, generous, thoughtful, and have great integrity.

Holland or the Netherlands—has been part of my life for a very long time. Very early on in my working days in London, I went over to Rotterdam on a work visit. I went there for the Society for the Promotion of Urban Renewal, to do an evaluation of one of the Rotterdam housing estates, called Pendrecht, so that we could compare their design approach to that used in progressive housing we were building in London, at the time. Other visits were with my wife to holiday in Amsterdam. Over time I met a number of Dutch planners, and through one of them—Frans, I was invited to come and spend one of my sabbatical leaves in the Netherlands. This leave was spent at T.N.O., which is the Dutch National Research Institute, based in Delft. In this institute was a special planning research centre where Frans worked, and where I was able to spend two and a half months, as a senior visiting researcher. This gave me the opportunity to look at how the whole systems of leisure provision, tourism development, and conservation functioned in the Netherlands, as well as helping in the translation of a range of documents that had been produced in Dutch, into English versions. As during this time I was going to stay alone, Frans and his wife Olga, invited me to be their guest, staying with them and their two children, in their home in Waddinxveen. The exciting thing about that stay, is that I was able to 'plug-in' to daily Dutch life. Thus, each morning after having a Dutch breakfast, I would join Frans, and go in a shared car which was part of a car-pool, that took us to and from work. At work one worked at a desk, with coffees being brought around, and at lunchtime you went to a canteen, where you had a standard Dutch researchers lunch! This was of Karnemelk and belegje brodjes (filled rolls). After lunch we would go into the leisure room, and play table tennis intensely for perhaps 15 or 20 minutes, before returning to office work.

Staying with Frans and his family was interesting, because one learnt about the complex local schooling, which seemed to have two streams—one state and secular, the other catholic. Secondly, one learned quite a lot about leisure patterns. Time was taken in the evenings and weekends to take the bikes and go cycling along the special cycle tracks through to local recreational areas, that had capacity to give enjoyment to thousands of local residents.

I found that both at work and at home, Dutch people tend to do things in groups, much more than the Brits do. A group would go together to the equivalent of a bar, or to a pancake-house, and it was unusual for two friends to do something together, as opposed to going off in a group of half a dozen people. Delft—where we worked, is a beautiful historic town, so sympathetic in scale, that you feel you can contain it in the palm of your hand, and can get to know it very well, and love it very quickly. Through Frans, I got to know another colleague at the Institute very well, his name was Dree, and he was a young married man, with his wife, with whom I quickly became friends. Frans came from a Rotterdam working class family, and I did eventually meet both his parents, as well as his in-laws, and that gave one another range of impressions. With Frans I went to various official meetings, both in different organisations in the Netherlands, as well as to one set of meetings at the European Commission in Brussels, thus we got to know each other very well, as well as getting to know his family.

Frans's marriage eventually broke-up, as a result of his involvement with another woman, Anka, whom he was later to marry, and settle down with, but this had complex consequences. The children stayed with Olga, and relations between former husband and wife were very difficult, and complex over questions of access to the children. Furthermore, Frans's second wife became ill on a long term basis, and it was very hard to know how far that illness was real or psychosomatic. Frans' second wife Anka, became extremely possessive, and rather suspicious. Thus it was difficult to speak to him on the phone in later years, and if you visited them she would always have to be present, in every conversation. You could not even go out to a bar for a drink, without her. This was all particularly strange, as at their request I had been Frans' best man at his second wedding. I had found that a somewhat difficult role, as I didn't want to be disloyal to his first wife. Sadly, because of the way over the years in which things deteriorated, we ceased to have contact with Frans and his second wife, and this was a matter of some sadness to me.

However, we do still have contact with Dree, and his wife—Mariet. They live in a very nice house in Delft South, but do not have any children. This was because of complex reasons, but they are a happy and fulfilled couple. Dree subsequently developed his own commercial firm, which until recently was doing very well, and his wife who was doing interesting and experimental nursing work in social institutions in the Rotterdam area. They are and remain strong and good friends. They come from the extreme South of the Netherlands, and speak a Dutch patois which sounds almost closer to German—than to standard Dutch. They are a lively, warm, kind, and generous couple, whose continuing friendship is important to us, as a family.

Over the years too other Dutch friends were made, with Michel—who worked in various Government Ministries, and lived with his girlfriend and their two children. A friendship which has ended, was with Cor, who was the senior partner in a major planning consultancy, and is now retired. Latterly, I was for several years lecturing at Dutch Tourism, Hotel, and Planning Schools located at Wageningen, Amsterdam, Breda, Tilburg, Rotterdam, Leeuwarden and The Hague. Regular lectures on this circuit was a source of great pleasure, and through them I became very friendly with Ton, who was in his second marriage to a wife, who was also in her second marriage. This is a close continuing friendship, which has led to frequent visits to see Ton and his wife in the Netherlands, and their reciprocal visits across here, to see us in the UK.

The links with countries like Belgium, have been far less fruitful in human terms. Many visits have related to visits to the European Commission, and later to the European Union in Brussels, or some on lecturing visits to either the Free University of Brussels, the University in Bruges, or the University in Louvain. I have had friendly relations with a number of people working at these institutions, but none of these have led to long term friendships, in the way that Danish and Dutch connections have done.

Norway and Sweden are two countries which I have regularly visited on lecture tours. In Norway I have been going to Olso, Lillehammer, Bergen, Trondheim, and further North. In Sweden, the lecture visits have basically been to two places—namely Ostersund and Falun-Borlange—this was because I had met the two people that ran these courses, namely Lars and Magnus, at a tourism course I had given years earlier at Dubrovnik, in what was then Federal Yugoslavia. In both these cases, the towns were in remoter rural Sweden. In the course of Norwegian visits there are three people I got to know well, firstly Sondre at Lillehammer, and secondly Jan Vidar—at a national research institute in Oslo. Through Sondre, I met Borge, who lived in a remote rural location in Norway. Sondre's wife is a famous painter and designer, who regularly represents Norway at all sorts of events at home and abroad, and Sondre himself has a very special character, as he comes from Telemark. Telemark is a different and special area. It contains a high frozen plateau—Hardangervidda, where the people have a very distinct character. They are quiet; they speak very slowly, and thoughtfully, and chew things over at length, before they come to opinions on anything.

Nyquist's 1979 book gives a good impression of the feeling of Hardangervidda. Through Sondre I got to know not only his University at Lillehammer, but him, his family and his friends, as well as the lovely traditional house in which they live in Lillehammer. I have hosted visits by Sondre and Borge to wilderness areas in Scotland,

and in return have had the pleasure of being hosted to visit great Norwegian wilderness areas, like the Hardangervidda. Sadly in 2012 I learned, belatedly, of Sondre's death.

Telemark and Hardangervidda are the areas where the heroes of Telemark fought during the Second World War, and where Norwegians tried to destroy the heavy water plant which the Germans had taken over during the war, and was to have been the basis on which the Nazi atomic bomb was to be developed. I had the opportunity on Norwegian visits, to see these extraordinary sites, works and even meet some of the people who've been involved in these amazing exploits. It is amazing to learn the stories of Norwegian underground actions during the Second World War. I have developed a love for Norway and its people, as well as for its landscapes, whereas I have very different feelings towards Sweden. Perhaps this is because in the Second World War, though the Swedes were supposedly neutral, they let the Nazi troops cross Sweden to invade Norway, an action which was hardly a neutral thing to do!

Libaek & Stenersen's 1995 History of Norway, is excellent for giving Norway's story clearly.

Perhaps the reference to the war, gives me an opportunity to bring in Germany, and my visits there. In the first place, many years ago, back in the 1950's when one could still go hitchhiking in Europe, my wife and I hitchhiked across France and Germany and were astounded to come across the frequent references by Germans, to the war. In those days everyone told us that they had nothing to do with the war, and had been conscientious objectors, so that after a week or two of such comments, we felt sorry for Hitler that he had so little support, apparently!

Later work visits involved links with planning schools, on the one hand, in the Saarland, and on the other—in Darmstadt. The most extraordinary visit was when I was invited by Internationes, which is the German equivalent of the British Council, to go on a study tour of Germany. There I was taken from city to city, meeting planning officers and research directors, all of whom would tell me about their glorious achievements in reconstruction since the Second World War. It was not until I reached Munich, that I walked into an office there, where my host was very different to everyone else whom I'd met before. He said "you look tired, do you want to sit down, and chat, or go out to a beer-garden and chat over a drink there?" We chatted in the beer garden, and that evening he invited me back to his home, where I had supper with him, his wife and children. This was my first contact with Gerhard, an extraordinary man, who has remained part of my life, to this day. Gerhard had been a fighter pilot with the Luftwaffe in the Second World War. He had been brought up through Hitler Youth and was a committed Nazi. It was not until the end of the war when he was a prisoner of war, and he saw his officers acting in ways that shocked him, that his whole system eventually crumbled, and he obviously spent a few years trying to sort himself out. Now he is a convinced pacifist, who spends much of his retirement time in Poland, and in Israel, trying to compensate to Poles on the one hand, and to Jews on the other, for the things that he did during the Second World War. He is that rare thing, a man of great honesty and integrity, who is trying to compensate for the things that he did, earlier in his life. Through Gerhard I got to understand the strengths and weaknesses of post-war German planning. There was an honesty in evaluation. and a closeness in discussion, which meant that not only did a professional link develop, but also a strong personal link, whereby on later work trips to Yugoslavia, Gerhard and his wife would join me. Or on a work trip to Turkey, Gerhard would team up with me. It's extraordinary how out of an unpromising and blatantly propagandist study tour, provided by Internationes, a very real and important personal friendship later developed.

One other friendship in Germany related to that with a Belgium architect, who married a German wife, and settled in a medium-sized city in Germany. Jean was an eco-architect before it was fashionable to be so, and he saw the need to create 'Green Buildings', that were energy efficient, and surrounded by gardens, that re-used and recycled old building materials and plant materials, in ways that were a model for others. His lectures at conferences, his book on recycling in gardens, were impressive, imaginative, and yet very practical. It's a source of great sadness that a few years ago this very talented Belgium architect, who settled in Germany, died suddenly, and I lost a friend of quality and integrity.

Though many work-visits over the years have been made to France, because of my work links with the O.E.C.D. in Paris, with the French Government, and with other international and French organisations, the relationships with most French professionals, whom I met, remained pleasant but superficial. The change, as far as France was concerned, occurred some years ago, when my wife and I went on holiday to Arcachon. Arcachon is a French resort for French tourists, and is located near to Bordeaux. I had first discovered it, on my 1951 hitchhiking trip to France, with Bimbo. Many years afterwards my wife and I decided to visit this resort, about which I had often spoken to her, but which we had not visited together. We stayed in a nice waterfront hotel in Arcachon, and over the first few days started to become friendly with a French family, dining daily at a nearby dining table, in the hotel. At this table there was a 16 year old young man, together with his grandparents. His parents, who were a Lawyer and a Pharmacist, could not make this holiday, so the grandparents had taken their lively grandson on holiday to Arcachon. As both my wife and I are French speakers, we first got into conversation with the grandson, and then later—the grandparents, and daily would have long chats with them, before one day joining them on a day visit to Chateau Margaux. This was a great day out, with a lot of fun, and humour. We understood the inherent conflicts between the grandparents and the grandson, and got to know them very well. We were subsequently invited to visit the missing parents of the young man, whose name was Francois. The way that things worked out, was that Francois actually first came on a visit of a few weeks to stay with us in Birmingham, supposedly to improve his English. However, what happened in that delightful stay, was that as he knew we were fluent French speakers, we switched to speaking French at home, for a few weeks.! We all had a great time together, and subsequently we were invited to meet his "missing parents" at their home in the Auvergne. Our visit to the Auvergne was an enormous success. We got on extremely well with the father and the mother, as well as by now being very close to the grandson, and fairly friendly with the grandparents, as well. Though nowadays we are only in touch as far as the exchange of Christmas cards and occasional emails are concerned, that deep connection with a French provincial family, was something rich, unexpected, and greatly valued.

Italy, Spain and Portugal are countries which we have grown to love, partly through holidays and partly through work visits. I have lectured at the University Tourism School in Rome two or three times, in Venice University—perhaps four times, as well as worked with research organisations in Madrid and Barcelona. The Italian work connection started when Alberto, a larger than life Italian academic, invited me to lecture at his tourism school in Rome. He is a wonderfully colourful character who will invite you out to splendid restaurants for wonderful meals, whereby you learn about Roman cuisine on one hand, or Sardinian on the other. In comparison, the deputy who runs the Venice Tourism School, Maria, is a first class academic, charming, lively, and rigorous, who has hosted work-visits, with small social elements in them to Oriago, where the school is located, found a little inland from Venice itself.

From these visits I developed a great love for Venice, though a growing sadness about its demise. This is because of its shrinking population, and the transfer of its workers to Mestre, across the lagoon, as Venice is left to die elegantly. Rome is a city which I got to know, but frankly do not like very much. There is something both about the character of Rome, and of its people which does not particularly appeal to me, although individual monuments, fountains and elements of the city may impress, but it is not a place in which you could easily feel at home. Nevertheless, through the visits arranged by Alberto, I sometimes did joint lecturing with my friend. a Professor from Vienna, called Jozef Mazanec, and that at least had the advantage that in free time he and I could go out on walks together, exploring the Apian Way, or small cafes—tucked away in the big city.

Earlier in the text I have referred to Spain, and there I've had three successive friends. One was named Pedro, a planner from Madrid, whose first marriage split up and who eventually went on working trips to South America, so we lost contact. Secondly there was Juan, who originally comes from Barcelona, but is now settled with his wife and son in Madrid. There he works in the computing field, but his real interests and passions are for painting and poetry. His 2003 book of poetry contains some memorable word images. He has painting exhibitions, and publishes books of his own poems, and he is someone with whom I remain regularly in touch, and occasionally see when we visit Madrid on holiday. Sadly, we have not as yet persuaded Juan to visit us in England, though we have had the pleasure of seeing Pedro here in the past. We have no remaining personal links in Portugal, which is an interesting country to visit, but frankly my preference is for Spain, as I speak Spanish and don't speak Portuguese, so I feel much more at home in Spain. There we can make our way round urban and rural areas, using Spanish and not having to rely on translation, which creates barriers with Spanish people. The Spanish have a particular character which I feel I understand, and with which I am at home, so it is always very easy to go to Spain, and feel part of the place. A third Spanish friend was met first in Poland, then again in Spain. He is an academic, teaching economics in Galicia, which is his home territory. Nowadays, my contact with Luis is mainly by email.

The visits to and links with Eastern Europe on the one hand, and the Balkans on the other, have been other strong elements, which I will tell more about—later in the book.

CHAPTER FOURTEEN

Polish re-connections, and Eastern Europe.

Though Rom Dylewski left London in 1960, it was not until 1962 that he persuaded us to go on our first visit to Poland. That was a big decision, as this was a time when Poland had a hard Communist system, that made life for foreign tourists complex and difficult. We had undertaken the sea journey up the Baltic to Gdynia–Gdansk, and even after our arrival we had the long train trip from Gdansk to Warsaw. It is important to remember that we were travelling with our one and a half year old daughter, and tackling a six–hour train journey with a small child, when no eating or drinking facilities were available aboard the Polish trains, made it very difficult for us.

Fortunately, Rom met us in Warsaw, and we were able to continue our travel with him by train and bus to our destination. In those days one had to register with the police every 24 hours, as well as paying a daily tourist tax, for the privilege of being in Poland! We stayed part of the time in the Dom Architecta in Kazimierz-Dolny, and part of the time in the Palace of Pulawy, which was the home of the Agricultural University, where the parents of Rom's wife—Jadwiga, lived. The period spent at the Dom Architecta (architects' home) was wonderful, as there was a fine mixture of impressive architects, artists, and writers staying there at the time. Thus picnics in the pine woods with such good company, or walks in and around the historic settlement of Kazimierz Dolny, were truly memorable events.

This was a difficult economic period, as well as being a complex political time—in Poland. Travel had to be by train and bus, as there were virtually no private cars in that country. Consumer goods were very restricted and limited in their availability. Personal freedoms were very limited, but annual holidays were available to all workers—via the system of provisions by trade unions and similar organisations. Wonderful and original craft pottery and naïve cut-out pictures were readily available, but choice in foods and drinks was very limited when you ate out at the co-operative cafes. In 1962 Polish towns and villages were still in the stage of reconstruction, necessary after the huge scale and disastrous impacts of the Second World War upon that country.

The Dylewski family in Lublin, Poland: Rom, Jadwiga, and their two children Syzmon and Magda.

Part of Tony's Polish Consulting Team, in a wintry Silesia, Poland, in the 1992-94 period.

Time spent in Poland in 1962 was both memorable, and gave both my wife and I a love of that country, with its beautiful landscapes, great rivers, historic towns, and impressive people whom we met. It also created the opportunity to reconnect with a country which had been my family's home for many hundreds of years, though this was a time when the vast majority of its previously large Jewish population had been ruthlessly exterminated during the Nazi occupation. The books by Vinecour 1977, Fuks 1988, and Webber 2009, together give an effective picture of the changed Jewish situation in Poland. Suddenly it was a Poland virtually without Jews, though their past presence was still evidenced by Jewish cemeteries, large former synagogues, and other monuments, that remained. I did not realise in 1962 that that visit was going to lead to along and complex continuing relationship for me—with the country of Poland.

Many more visits to Poland were made after 1962, some for work reasons, and others for personal reasons. The work trips included taking Scottish planning students by train across Europe to Poland, and giving them an exposure to the planning and reconstruction systems that had been used in that country. Some trips were to Warsaw, to lecture in planning at the Institut Francais, on behalf of the University of Bordeaux. Other visits were to holiday in the Tatra Mountains in the South of Poland, or to stay on the Hel Peninsula, in the extreme north of the country, by the Baltic Sea. These series of visits gave opportunities to get to know more of the country, as well as to get acquainted with Polish students, in their own country. On one visit with a group of British students from the London area, I got to know a young Polish doctor, who was also a Tatra guide, and he—Wiktor Siegel, was—over time to become a close friend.

What was unexpected was that in the 1990's, I was invited there to take a senior post in a consultancy that was to do work for the European Union, in Poland. This was in 1992, some 30 years after my first visit to that country, when I became Project Director for the PHARE Tourism Development Programme, based in Warsaw, and thus living in the city which my grandpa had escaped from in his youth, to avoid czarist conscription! Though my contract was for a two year period, it ended after 15 months due to major health problems, and complex management and other issues in this programme. It gave me the opportunity to create two successive homes in Warsaw, to work with an excellent young team of Polish colleagues, one of whom—Magda, was my counterpart officer.

During this time in Poland I was fortunate enough to have a whole sequence of visitors, including my wife, my daughter, as well as a range of friends. These included Paddy, Mark, and Richard from England, Marko from Slovenia, Zoran from Croatia, Ton from the Netherlands, plus Milt and Barb from the USA. Most of all, this time gave the opportunity to reconnect with the family's roots in Warsaw. Thus, on a Sunday I was able to spend the time as my grandfather had done in his youth, strolling in the Lazienki Palace Gardens, listening to the outdoor Chopin concert there, and taking coffee and cakes in the small café in the park. The work aspects of this visit have been dealt with in my first book, so I will not deal with them here. However, what was fascinating was that this was the period of changeover from communism to a mixed economy, in Poland, and so many aspects of this process were intriguing, puzzling, and at times surprising!

The visits to Poland were part of a remarkable familiarisation which I gained between the 1970's and the 2000's, with much of Eastern Europe. This included getting to know not only Slav societies, but also Latin cultures—such as that of Romania, and complex different cultures such as those of Hungary on the one hand, and Estonia-on the other. The visit to Romania was complex one in which I was doing an evaluation of the effects of European aid programmes to that country, so had the opportunity to travel widely within it, and get to know something of that fascinating and varied nation, whose people are so different to their slav neighbours. The mountains, ski resorts, and historic monasteries were unexpected delights to explore, and I met some extremely impressive Romanians during this visit.

One of them was a young man—named Cosmin, who aided me in some of my work, spoke good English, was helpful and adaptable, and unexpectedly became a friend over time. I was able to give him the opportunity to visit England, and both to do some work with me here in the UK, as well as in the Netherlands. Equally friends were made in slav countries such as Bulgaria, where I got to know Ivo, and Slovakia, where my friendship with Rudi Aroch, and later with his son young Rudi Aroch, gave a continuity of personal connection over a long period. On my first visit to Bratislava, I was struck by his wonderful sense of humour, which showed me how intelligent East Europeans survived crazy political situations! One day, standing with me on the banks of the River Danube, Rudi pointed to all the barbed wire along the international frontier, the searchlights, the machine gun nests, and said to me . . .

"Don't you find it difficult to live in the West, behind all that barbed wire, searchlights and guns?!"

Thus I learned of the way of survival that East Europeans developed, to cope with the communist system, and periods of Russian occupation of their countries.

Time spent in Romania, Slovakia, Bulgaria, and the Czech Republic, all gave opportunities to get to know richly civilised countries, with extraordinary histories, resilient people, and a variety of experiences which made me feel committed to, and deeply interested in them and their peoples. The DDR—or East Germany, on the one hand, and Estonia on the other, were amongst the most complex to deal with, as the DDR was a brutally controlled state, and Estonia—the Baltic state with a long historic identity, was being Russianised, and suppressed, despite its strong linguistic and cultural identity. Sadly my work in Estonia was damaged by the actions and dishonesty of my French working host there, which left both a sick taste in my mouth, as well as colouring my personal impressions of a particular place, namely the lovely historic capital city of Tallinn.

Central and Eastern Europe still generate mixed responses on my part—for a variety of reasons. Hungary, which is a very interesting country not only for its capital city—Budapest, but also its great Lake Balaton, is a frustrating place because of its impenetrable language! Hungarian is not a language that the visitor can casually acquire, in the way that one can quickly gain a smattering of language in the Latin and Slav cultures. Austria is a central European country to which I have made a number of working visits, especially to Vienna and Salzburg. However, the associations with these visits are not generally happy ones, for though I speak a basic German, on three occasions I have experienced neo-Nazi outbursts, that shocked me, and still make me feel ill at ease about that country and its people. The exception is one good friend who long worked in Vienna, but whose family was Czech in origin, his name is Jozef, and he is one of the finest academics, and human beings whom I know.

One central European country to which I have not yet referred is Switzerland, where I spent 5 or 6 weeks lecturing at a hotel school, and have also lectured at Swiss Universities. Whilst I do not like making generalisations, I did find that the extraordinarily fine Swiss landscapes would seem to merit a better people than the Swiss. Swiss neutrality seems to have been used to hide crude self interest, passive support for Nazism, and obsessions with money and materialism which dominate social discussions, among even academics there! Exceptions prove the rule, they say, and one Swiss Italian friend I have—named Ezra, is the most altruistic and non-materialist person I have ever met!

Poland and East European connections have been very important to me, and there are still many individual friends who live in those countries, and whose friendship I value greatly. My love of Poland in particular, is still real and continuing, and it is a source of considerable regret that my current health condition prevents me from spending more time there now.

CHAPTER FIFTEEN

National scandal in
Newcastle upon Tyne

The move from London to Newcastle upon Tyne was a very complex one. Before I had taken the post my mentor—Prof. Holliday, had warned me not to join the small team of an engineer, as he believed that only architect-planners were capable of good city-planning. However, my own meeting with Wilf Burns, the engineer who was to be the new city planner of Newcastle upon Tyne, led to my believing in him, and wanting to join his team. The place—Tyneside, with Newcastle as its crowning glory, was both an intriguing and appealing one. It is a mini-conurbation, focused on the River Tyne, isolated from other areas, and with strong cultural, physical and linguistic characteristics, which give it great appeal. The new city planning department was to be a test case for planning, as the Labour Councillor Dan Smith—who chaired the city's Planning Committee, was staking his reputation on this risky venture, which was to be tested out for a six-month period, in the first instance! This meant that the young team leaders, like myself, who were coming anew to this area, were taking a great risk in accepting six-month contracts, and no promise of work security.

What we as a team believed, however, was that thoughtful, sensitive, Geddesian planning could change and aid the fate of such urban-regions, that had never benefitted from such planning. It was a risky business, as I was a young professional man. with a wife and a six week old daughter, coming to a place where we had few links, no security, but a belief that we could make change to and for local people, here in Newcastle upon Tyne. From my initial talks with both Wilf Burns—who was my boss, and with Dan Smith—who effectively was my employer, these were people in whom I believed, whom I trusted, and with whom I was keen to work on the Tyneside Crusade! From my knowledge of Wilf Burns' work in Coventry, I knew that we both shared a similar approach to strategic planning, whereby policies would be based on vital research, and the planning might prove different to what others were doing elsewhere in the country.

Model of Central Newcastle upon Tyne Planned Redevelopment, in the 1960's.

We were a small team initially of perhaps 12 or 14 people, doing work which later required the involvement of a team of 60! Thus we had to work very long hours, in order to achieve in 6 months, what others in much larger teams would have demanded some 2 years to do. As the Research Officer for this new department, I had an exceptionally heavy work-load, as I needed to lay the foundations for a review of the city development plan, review housing policy, transport policies, economic policies, social policies and even arts policies!

Whist Tyneside was essentially a left-wing area, the city of Newcastle upon Tyne was a place which was a tipping-point between Left and Right, so that sometimes it was Labour, and sometimes Conservative. The Dan Smith era, was one when the city had tipped in the Labour direction, but one did not know how long it would stay that way! All sorts of forces were at work in the background, and early on, one became aware of some curious individuals and agencies, who were at work. Some of the local politicians—both on the right and on the left, were somewhat dubious in terms of their morality, and a few months after starting work in Newcastle, there were large private lunches being offered in a major central hotel, by unknown parties, to which officers of the new city planning department, were invited. I went to only one such lunch, where it was clear to me that there were hidden agendas involved, and our unknown hosts, were plying us with drink to such an extent, that I quickly changed to drinking water, and made sure that I went to no such further lunches! Over time it became clear that investment groups, pressure groups, and some crooked politicians were involved. using the changes in the city as bases for their own aggrandisement. Later, the so-called Poulson Affair revealed the nature of this ongoing scandal, but—as is often the case in such events, the minor players tend to get caught, and some of the big players go free. Based on all that I saw, Cllr. Dan Smith was such a minor player, who was committed totally to trying to help his city, and his personal financial failures were of a very modest nature, and it is very sad to see how he was victimised, and suffered, compared to some of the bigger players, who were let off scot free.

The new city planning department and its staff—had four, six-month contracts, over which time it carried out an enormous programme of work. It stopped the process of total demolition which was being carried out on the city's housing stock, and re-evaluated housing condition, whereby it reached the view that the city's 73,000 houses basically needed modernising, and "enveloping", not demolition. Thus an urban housing rehabilitation programme, was initiated in Newcastle, on a scale which was unprecedented in the UK. Similarly, with regard to unemployment, radical policies were initiated. Tyneside had historically relied on ship-building, coal-mining, and other old industries which were now dying, and new sources of employment had to be created on a large scale. Thus I became involved in negotiations in many spheres, ranging from new office investment, to improvement in air and rail communications to and in the North East. The renewal of the city centre, its pedestrianisation, and efforts to renew the Quayside area of the city, were other major work tasks as well. All this work required very long work hours, and this led to great conflicts between one's work and personal life. My wife, daughter and I had moved into a rented flat in Whitley Bay, which seemed a pleasant seaside suburb. As I was out at work for long hours this left my wife coping with a young baby, in a flat, with no friends nearby, with an outlook over a small cemetery, and no social or familial support locally. It was all at a cost, and led to my wife having problems with post-natal depression, and becoming seriously ill—trying to cope with that situation.

A major contrast between work at the LCC in London, and work in Newcastle upon Tyne, was that in London we had been part of a very large international team, but in the North-East the teams were small and all—British. My immediate boss was Ken Galley—an able, likeable, dour, Yorkshireman, and my immediate partner on the development plan work was David Lloyd from Chichester. Ken's Austrian wife—Herta, was the only non-Brit in our wider entourage. In a two-year period the Newcastle upon Tyne City Planning Department justified itself, and became a long life feature of the city's administration. We completed the full first review of the city development plan, implemented changed city-wide housing policy, did a major review of employment, reviewed air transport, and developed the city's airport, implemented the urban motorway programme, and the pedestrianisation of the city centre, established regional arts policy, and did the first social policy studies in the city, relating to prostitution, social deprivation, and access to facilities. Professionally, this period was one of fulfilment and success, but it was all at a cost personally and in family terms. Philippa had a long period of serious illness based in hospital in Newcastle upon Tyne, during which we had moved to a semi-detached house in Brunton Park, north of Gosforth, where we lived around the corner from Philippa's old friend—Judy Lion. During this period my mother came up from Cardiff to look after my daughter Abigail, whilst Philippa was in hospital. As a result of the domestic circumstances of my Tyneside work period, we decided to move southwards, and an opportunity came to move to Birmingham, where I was offered a lectureship in the School of Planning, at the Birmingham College of Art. There I hoped to be able to combine lecturing with more time spent with my wife and daughter, in a larger Jewish community, where I hoped they would be happy and well. Little did I know of all the work pressures that the new job would involve, but we started off well, when my Professor's son—John, invited Philippa, Abby, and myself to stay with them in their lovely Edgbaston home, whilst we house-hunted in Birmingham. It was an encouraging start to a new period in our mobile lives!

The work pressure in Newcastle was very great, and there was a lack of time for social activity. In the two-year period there, I had one brief sailing trip out of Tynemouth, a day's sailing at Beadnall, and a hill-walking trip up in the Cheviot Hills, with the Lion family. Tyneside is a wonderful place of great character and identity, which it was special to have worked in, but the domestic consequences of that time had a sad colouring effect upon our personal lives. It was only years later, when we were working and living in Edinburgh, that opportunities occurred to visit Northumberland and spend some time enjoying both its wonderful uplands, and its unspoilt coast. That is another story to which we will return at a later point.

CHAPTER SIXTEEN

"I don't hold with titles";
The Inner and Outer Hebrides.

As already indicated, the eight years spent living and working in Edinburgh were a "high" for me. The mixture of teaching, applied research, development and expansion of the planning school, launching of a doctoral programme, my growing involvement with the National Trust for Scotland, and the Scottish Branch of the Royal Town Planning Institute, plus a rich family life, with the birth of our third child—Alexander, was totally a heady mix!

The incident took place in 1969, when I was working with my team from the planning school, upon the Clyde study for the Scottish Tourist Board. It became necessary for me to meet with the Marquis of Bute, at his island ancestral home—Mount Stuart. I was expecting to meet an elderly & stuffy aristocrat, and he was expecting to meet a decrepit academic. Thus it was a great surprise, to discover that we were both roughly of the same age. At that time I was a radical young academic, and was not looking forward to meeting what I expected to be a crusty old Tory!

But when we met, my first statement to him was: "I don't hold with titles!" to which he replied: "neither do I, my name is John, what do I call you?". Thus opened one of the most interesting contacts in my life, namely that with John, the Marquis of Bute. It was an exciting time in several senses, as the Scottish Tourist Board was still a voluntary sector organisation, and our team at the Edinburgh College of Art and the Herriot Watt University was a new, young, growing, and enthusiastic one.

This key meeting with John Bute, was an important one, because it was the start of a valued friendship, and of a state of mutual respect between the two of us. Through our work on the Clyde, I became increasingly associated with John Bute at the National Trust for Scotland–where he was Chairman of that organisation. This was to lead on to our joint tours of the Scottish new towns, official visits to Orkney, and to Shetland, as well as joint visits to coastal areas—to examine the impacts of potential North Sea oil development. I came to appreciate what a dedicated conservationist he was, a model landlord of the island, an innovative developer of new industries, and skilled Chairman. Far too many people did not recognise all these fine qualities of John's, far greater than his civilised charm. Drummond's 1996 collection of tributes to John Bute give a good idea of the wide range of John's work activities, and his personal attributes. John's right-hand man at the NTS, was Jamie Stormonth Darling, another person, whose skills and abilities I came to regard very highly.

I soon realised that the island of Bute is in the Inner Hebrides of Scotland, and that I had an inherent feel for both the Inner and Outer isles. Tobermory, on the Isle of Mull is, where we chose to go for our honeymoon, and I recalled that Patrick MacAskill, the great influence upon me in New Zealand, had himself come from the Isle of Lewis, in the Outer Hebrides. It was he who had Inculcated in me my love of Scotland, whilst in New Zealand, and had given me an appreciation of the special character of islands.

John, the Sixth Marquis of Bute.

Cruising with John and Jennifer, and their friends, on King Duck, on Loch Long, Scotland, 1972.

Touring Orkney and the Shetlands with John Bute, 1971.

The Author (far left) with part of his growing academic team at the Edinburgh College of Art's Planning School, by its Manor Place premises, in about 1967/68.

It was some considerable time, before I at last succeeded in making my 1st visit to the Outer Hebrides—or to the long Isle, as it is as it is known by the locals. That was the week which I spent together with Michael Dower, whom I had first met at the LCC, in London, and it was a rich and memorable time, including visits to Highland shows, standing stones, climbing Mt. Clisham–the highest peak in the Hebrides, and visiting remote crofts. That visit gave me an affection for the Outer Hebrides, one that I later found I shared with a new friend—the author–Robert Macfarlane. Robert Macfarlane & Roger Deakin's books on 'wild places' only recently discovered by me, are a source of great pleasure and stimulus.

The 1969/70 period, whilst working on the Clyde report, gave opportunities to get to know the islands of Bute and of Arran, both with members of the Clyde team, as well as with Scots friends, such as John Fullerton. It was a period as well when I made visits to the Highlands and Islands with Thomas Huxley, and other Edinburgh colleagues. This was a time when my passion for the islands, was added to my love of Highlands.

This love of islands, is something which had been developing over a long period, and had deepened as I had got to know the Yugoslav islands of the Adriatic, the Greek islands, and was later to get to know Island groups–such as the Balearics in the Western Mediterranean, the Canaries in the North Atlantic, the Hong Kong Island group, and the large island of Cyprus, in the Eastern Mediterranean. Holidays we spent on Gran Canaria, in the Canaries, on the island of Lesbos with the Greek planner—Takis Komilis and his wife, and on the island of Majorca, all reinforced this love of islands which has grown over a lifetime.

If it is hard to know whether the love of mountains and wilderness, with their special appeal, is greater as an attraction than that of Islands, but it suffices to say that it is one of the great riches in life, that both sets of natural resources are there for us to enjoy and protect! The inner and Outer Hebrides are a wonderful, and accessible set of islands, which are virtually on our doorstep, and are all the more to be valued and appreciated, for their accessibility.

CHAPTER SEVENTEEN

Balkans and Islands Connections

My connections to the Balkans peninsula started in the later 1960s, when I was based in Edinburgh, and the opportunity occurred to collaborate on a tri-national study in the Istrian uplands of Yugoslavia. As head of the Edinburgh College of Art planning school, I started this work cooperation with the Darmstadt School of planning in Germany, headed by Prof Tom Sieverts, and the Zagreb University School of Planning under Prof Millic. Istria is an upland region which had been part of Italy until the end of the Second World War, when it was returned to Federal Yugoslavia. However, this upland region of small hill towns had lost most of its population, and had lost its economic functions, therefore the Yugoslavs were keen to see it renovated, resettled, and given a new lease of economic life. We embarked upon a joint work programme with 3 working languages–Croat, English, and German. To add to the complexity of the sub region, it included the town of Pazin, where the local headquarters of the Communist Party was based, so that we were all carefully supervised in terms of the political implications of all our actions. As at that time there was an American–Yugoslav program underway, there was great concern to see that we had no connections with the CIA, or any other American political agencies.

Whilst technically this became a demanding but worthwhile programme, it had extra dimensions of stress, because I—as the programme coordinator, had regularly to visit Pazin, to be interrogated by the Communist commissar for this area. The strains and pressures were so great, that I eventually finished up having to receive medical treatment at the regional hospital in Pula, which was some distance away. At the end of this work programme I was so exhausted, and rundown, that the hospital doctors recommended that I be driven back in my vehicle, with my visiting family—to Scotland, and that I should avoid in future ever working again in stressful Federal Yugoslavia!

For years afterwards, I assumed that I would have no further contact with Federal Yugoslavia, and the Balkans peninsula, as the work time there had proved so traumatic for me. Nevertheless, one-day an academic visitor from Croatia, who was visiting Aston University in Birmingham, came to visit me at University of Birmingham, where I now held the chair and the directorship of the Centre for Urban Studies. The visitor's name was Miro Dragicevic, and he was from the Institute of Tourism Research at Zagreb, in the Croatian part of Federal Yugoslavia. Our long and fruitful talks, led on to a visit to Birmingham from that institute's director, namely Prof Syrdan Markovic. This in turn led to his inviting me to come and lecture and have discussions at the Institute in Zagreb, where I became a regular visitor. Thus the reconnection to Federal Yugoslavia was established. My working links with the Zagreb Institute became both regular and strong, leading to my getting to know the work team there very well, and consequently getting involved in work projects that related to the island of Vis, as well as my wife and I are spending a holiday partly on the island of Mljet, and partly in the historic city of Dubrovnik, with the Dragicevic family. In this way I got to know parts of mainland Croatia, and a number of the Adriatic islands, which has such enormous appeal. My friendship with Miro, and Syrdan, extended to include Zoran Klaric, and other colleagues at the Institute.

Some years later I had a phone call from Braco Music, whom I had known long ago in Istria, and who was looking for a suitable UK academic department in which to place a Slovene planner/researcher, to gain experience of the British approach to tourism

Braco, Boris, Andrej and Marko—all from Slovenia

*A montage of personal connections in the Balkans—including those in Slovenia, Croatia, Serbia, Romania and Geece.

Takis and Zak, from Greece   Zoran and Miro, fom Croatia

Cosmin from Romania   Aleksander from Serbia

development planning. To cut a long story short, this resulted in the visit to Birmingham by Marko Koscak, a Slovene engineer planner, who spent several months with me in Birmingham, and travelling round the UK, on a personalised program of intensive study. This all worked out very well, proved to be an effective and useful time of study, and lead on to my being invited on working visits to Slovenia, and collaboration there not only with Marko, but also with Prof Boris Leskovec, head of architecture at the Ljubljana University Department, and with Slovene government ministries. My links with Boris, resulted in my involvement in a special programme of work on the Island of Unije, where a Finnish/Slovene programme of cooperation was being conducted. Thus over time I found that my Federal Yugoslav connection extended from work in Croatian Istria, Zagreb, Slovenia, and later Dubrovnik, where I started to do tourism lectures on their international tourism program. As Croat islands had also been visited, my knowledge was rapidly extending both of the mainland, and of the Adriatic island system. Over time too, friendships evolved with two of Slovenia's best-known musicians–Andrej Pompe, band-leader, and the ballad singer—Alexander Mezek, and this gave an extra and special new dimension to the Yugoslav connection. The Civil War and the split-up of the former Federal Yugoslavia, was an event of special sadness for me, as I had believed in that Federal idea as the answer to that nation's problems, so that the loss of life, destruction, and suspicion which followed on from that phase, was very distressing.

Quite separate from the Yugoslav connection, has been my long connection with Greece. In my Manchester University days, I knew two Greek architect students in Manchester, and both in Edinburgh and Birmingham had connections with the planning, and tourism schools in Athens, from which we had a regular flow of Greek students to our departments in the UK. From 1973 onwards there was a steady flow of Greek students to Birmingham, and I had close connections with at least 3 of these students. Constantinos–was the son of an Athens hotelier, whom I got to know well both in Birmingham and in Athens, where I went to attend an international tourism conference. Sadly, this very talented young man died in his 20's whilst he was serving in the Greek Navy, dived from a boat, and never surfaced again. Fouli is a very talented woman who did her doctorate in Birmingham University, and is a professional of great ability, initiative, and imagination. She returned to Greece as an adviser to a Greek Prime Minister, and has since established an international reputation for herself as a tourism consultant, at a world scale. Two of her friends and contemporaries from Athens, were students at the same time as her, in Birmingham. They were Kostas, and his sister. She completed her studies here, but Kostas did not, for complex personal and professional reasons. I saw him a few times in Athens, and was eventually able to find him a suitable post in Ireland, after he despaired about the corruption, and professional problems in Athens. I'm happy to say he is now personally and professionally well settled in the West of Ireland.

One professional contact whom I had in Greece was Takis Komilis, who worked for the economic planning agency (Kepe), was a highly skilled tourism planner, who had trained at Strathclyde University in Scotland, and with whom I had working contact over several years. He and his wife invited my wife and myself to holiday with them on the island of Lesbos, where he came from, and had his holiday home. This was one of the most delightful holidays which we have had, and enabled us to get to know an island which is off the beaten track, and is a fascinating, and varied place. Takis loaned us his architect-sister's home, opposite his own, where we could sit on the terrace under the grapes, and read, or look out to sea, in an idyllic setting. I'm very sorry to say that a few years ago, first his wife, then later he died, and this was news that we received with great sadness.

A few years ago, when I was giving one of my occasional lectures to the tourism school at University College in Birmingham, a Greek student came up to me after my lecture to say he'd like to speak further to me about my work. We had a number of discussions, and I became his tutor whilst he was finishing his thesis at the college, before returning to Greece. I gave him the opportunity to work with me on one Balkans project, and he later invited both my wife and myself to come and visit his family, who were hoteliers near the historic site of Meteora, in northern Greece, in the town of Kalampaka. Zak–his first name, became a close friend of the family, and I'm delighted to say we still have regular visits from him in Birmingham, as he comes over specially from Greece to keep in touch with us.

In the Balkans context I have already separately referred to my visits to Bulgaria, and Romania. A country to which I have not yet referred is Albania, which I visited for work and a visit on behalf of the United Nations Priority Actions Programme. I went on a joint visit there with Dr Zoran Klaric, to examine and evaluate a first possible site for a new Seaside resort on the coast, near the main seaport of that country. Albania is a grossly underdeveloped country which has suffered from both Communist and right wing governments, and it is in a parlous state, due to the waste of public monies on big, crazy, defence projects, and development plans that never became reality. The local people with whom I worked were unimpressive, the evidence of poverty, and corruption was disturbing, and I left the country with an enormous feeling of frustration, as so much needed doing that you felt would never be done. To my mind, Albania is a Balkan tragedy.

The last of my Balkan visits was to a country which I had never before visited, namely Serbia. I was invited there with my colleague and friend Marko, from Slovenia, in order to carry out a special sub regional study on South West Serbia, an underdeveloped area with great scenic, wildlife, and other natural resources, which give it great potential for eco-tourism development. We worked there with Aleksandar Marinkovic–an excellent Serbian planner, who was known to Marko, and also became a friend of mine. This underdeveloped part of Serbia is partly Islamic, and partly Christian, and this divide, plus lack of Central government investment, leaves this attractive area, which has much potential, in a continuing underdeveloped State. As a team we worked hard and creatively to produce a thoughtful, useful and practical plan, which sadly will never be implemented, though it could have formed a sound base for the area's future.

The Balkans, and Balkanisation many sadly continue to be the state of this wonderful, mountainous peninsula, with its great diversity, divisions, suspicions and myopic attitudes that will prevent it from ever realising it's many potentials. The islands of the Adriatic are vast in number, and greatly varied in their condition and character, due to variable rainfall levels, settlement levels, and varied histories. Some–especially in the North Adriatic, places like Losinj, are already highly developed touristically, and will continue to attract European tourists because of there are enormous appeal and accessibility.

CHAPTER EIGHTEEN

Deep in Darkest Detroit

It is paradoxical that the way to Detroit, was via Salzburg, in Austria. In 1969 I was invited with about 60 other European planners to attend an American urban seminar, which was held for a month in Schloss Leopoldskron, in Salzburg. That was an extraordinary Winter experience, in the great Palace that had been used for the filming of "the Sound of Music", where we attended lectures and seminars, and between snowstorms went on trips out into the Salzgammergut. The Seminar was used to select people for the International programme which had started in the Centre for Urban Studies, at Wayne State University, in Detroit USA. In 1970 my family and I flew from Edinburgh to Detroit, where I was to be employed for a semester, as a senior research fellow on that new program.

Detroit is a virtually unknown American metropolis, from a European viewpoint except perhaps for two images–of it being the U.S. Motown, the place which makes cars, and as the home of soul music! Therefore, perhaps it would be useful to introduce that exotic and unknown Metropolis, with a summary profile of its historical development.

Detroit was founded as a French settlement in the year 1701. It was then that Antoine Cadillac established" Fort Pontchartrain du Detroit" on the broad straight that connects Lake St Clair, and Lake Erie. This was a settlement which was to go through French, British, and American occupations. It grew slowly in the 19th century, until railroad building came in the 1850's, by which time Detroit already had its fine villas, and public buildings. By 1860 Detroit had a recorded population of 45,600 residents. By the 1870s it was acquiring some major urban characteristics–the City Hall was built in 1871, an opera house in 1872, and a major public library in 1877. The State of Michigan it self, became really established in the 1870s, when the Michigan State Capital was built in Lansing, in 1878! (see Hawkins-Ferry,1968).

From 1872 to1890 the Detroit region had an increasingly important industrial role, with copper and iron production, railroad car Manufacturing, to be followed by the vital start of car production from 1908 onwards. By 1890 the population of Detroit had reached 205, 876. This was the decade which 1st saw skyscrapers being built in the city, the human diversity of the population became ever richer. 1908 to 1921 was the period when big car factories were built in Detroit, and these included Chrysler, Ford, Dodge, Packard, and General Motors. Reflecting these and other car plant developments, the city's population reached 993,678 by 1920, and passed the million mark later in that decade. In 1922 the General Motors building, providing a headquarters for that organisation was built in Detroit, and the metro region was into a major expansion phase. In 1939 the Huron Clinton Metropolitan Parks authority was created for the region, which also developed a plan for its freeways in 1943, and a fully fledged campus project for Wayne State University in 1948.

Wartime expansion of industrial production in the 1940s saw bombers, tanks, as well as cars and trucks being produced in Detroit, in enormous numbers. This led to a labour shortage in the city, as a result of which a large-scale Black labour force was introduced from the South of the USA. Thus from 1940 to 1960 Detroit's black population rose from 9% to 29% of the total and in the post-war era Detroit became 40% black. Thus Detroit changed from being a White city in the 1870s, to being nearly half Black by the 1960s. By the 1960s there was a population of 4,176,000 living in the 5 County Detroit city region. By then the city was one of the most diverse in the USA, including 200,000 Poles, 150,000 Italians, 100,000 Ukrainians, plus substantial German, Jewish, Irish, Greek, Hungarian, minorities. Poor Appalachian migrants–both black-and-white, were flooding into the inner-city, at a time of economic recession.

Thus it was in the 1969/70 period, when we came to Detroit that the city which had been through its boom times in the 1940s, and the post-war consumer phase, was now in decline, had great problems of poverty and crime in the inner-city, and was suffering from race riots, and the nightly burning down of streets of residential properties, at the time we first arrived in this unknown city! When we arrived at the University Motel, located in the inner-city, the woman who was the manager proprietor, tried to reassure us that "don't worry honey, we've got police protection here, and they won't burn us down!" According to the local radio station, fires were burning on 7th and 8th streets, and police were clashing with rioters, downtown.

It was with some relief, that we had pre-planned a vacation in the Canadian Rockies, before we settled down in Detroit, so that very shortly afterwards, we flew on to Calgary in Alberta, for the start of a month's memorable holiday in the national parks of Jasper, Banff, Kootenay, and Yoho. From the time of our hiring the camper truck, setting off into the Rockies and staying at a set of fabulous campsites in the national parks, my wife and I and our three children knew that this was the ideal place for a contrasting

Life-long Michigan friends, first met in Detroit—Milt and Barb, (to the left) dining with us at the George Inn, Southwark, in London.

holiday to Detroit! Mountains, Lakes, glaciers, and forests presented us with a perfect holiday environment, and in addition we were able to spend part of our vacation with friends such as the Rogers family in the Okenagon Valley, and later stay at the home of my uncle Arnold, a member of the Seligman family, who lived in Vancouver, plus a stay with our American friends–the Tamarins, in the delightful U.S. city of Seattle.

At the end of the vacation we returned to Detroit, for a very different experience. The faculty at the Centre for Urban Studies was half black and half white. The white faculty were welcoming, but the black faculty were hostile, as this was a period when they did not wish to collaborate with whites, and were introverted both in social and work terms. We were living in an apartment block called the Belcrest, which had a faded gentility, and where we were somewhat crowded into a two-bedroom apartment for the 5 of us. Schooling was a priority need for our two older children, and this was a problem in Detroit. The inner-city schools were almost totally Black, the outer suburban schools almost totally white and by 1970 there was only one integrated school, namely in Lafayette Park. This was a special urban renewal area designed by Mies van der Rohe, and housing a mixed black-and-white, middle-class, group of residents. After much pressure, and a big battle I did succeed in getting our 2 older children into the integrated school, and this gave them a very special experience in Detroit terms. Characteristically, in December the school offered three alternative celebrations: a traditional Christmas for the white Christian kids, a Soul Xmas for the black kids, and a Chanucah celebration for the Jewish kids. Thus the three sets of middle class kids could each have their specific needs met!

Of the white faculty, my boss was Prof Jack Fisher, an extraordinary guy who specialised in Poland and Yugoslavia, spoke fluent Polish and Serbo-Croat, and was suspected by some of being a CIA agent! His assistant–Henry Henderson, is a Bostonian, who was an enormous help not only to ourselves, but also to a team of young European fellows, who would be joining us in this Detroit period. The Europeans were a lively young team from France, Switzerland, and Yugoslavia, and we all enjoyed doing our shopping together at the Eastern market, going on picnics, and working well and easily together. Some of the visiting faculty at the centre were particularly lively and interesting, and one of them Prof Bill Cooper, from Michigan State University specialised in applied ecology, and became a valued colleague and friend. We also became friendly with two of the planning staff in the city planning department—namely Milton Rohwer, and Doug Wonderlic. Milt, and his second wife—Barb, remain close friends to this day. When taking the children to play in the park one day at Lafayette Park, we met a young medical family from Seattle, who lived nearby and invited us to lunch. As a result of what became a friendship with that family they loaned us their spare car–which was a new Mustang, whose use in our free time positively transformed our lives in Detroit.

The conflicts in the Detroit Urban Studies Centre were in contrast to the vital growth and co-operation in my own new Department in Edinburgh. For my research at Wayne State I had to try out two topics; 1st I wanted to-do interviewing with the car workers who were members of the union of automobile workers (UAW), but they were on strike at the time, so this was not possible. My 2nd topic was to look at the character, functioning and evaluation of the Huron Clinton Metropolitan Parks Authority, and this proved to be possible. It became the very interesting basis of work then, and was supplemented by my lecture trips to a number of universities and colleges elsewhere in the USA. Thus I visited the University of Chicago, the University of California at Berkeley,(where I visited friends—like Profs, Jack Dyckman and Don Foley), the University of Illinois at Urbana, and Wesleyan Methodist College in Ohio. Both as a family, and individually we had many interesting experiences during our stay in Greater Detroit, and received some very warm hospitality especially from a range of white residents whom we met whilst we were living there.

Later other North American trips became possible; on one I led a team of British tourism specialists—to New York, to Washington DC, and to Virginia, and on other occasions–due to our elder son marrying an American bride, we had a wedding in New Jersey, a visit the Travis family in New York, a holiday on Cape Cod—in New England, and memorable meetings with old friends in New York and Boston. At the end of our time in Detroit, we spent Christmas partly in a friend's house in Lafayette Park in Detroit, and partly in the deep snows of Montréal, which is a fascinating city. Years later I was able to go on a three-week working visit to Quebec, having to speak French most of the time, as my hosts were speakers of Quebecqoise, in Montréal, Quebec, and Trois Rivieres. There is a vitality in the French-speaking province of Quebec, and visits there have proved to be enormously interesting and stimulating.

I'm very pleased that it was Detroit, and not some verdant campus in Virginia to which we went, for our American campus experience. I must comment upon the material generosity of the white Americans whom we met—both Christian and Jewish, their generous loans of their homes, and of their cars, the hosting of Thanksgiving dinners, welcoming lunches, and other features are memorable. The vitality of Detroit, it's fascinating mix of people, its jazz nights in offbeat urban dives, its problems and challenges, made it a singularly worthwhile semester in a truly American city. There is sadness for me in the non-response, and unfriendliness of American blacks met in the 1969/70 period. Perhaps this was a product of a specific time, and of history, but it was nevertheless really disappointing. Combining depressed Detroit with visits to the wonderful North American National Parks, gave one what was at times a "heaven and hell" contrast experience! Sadly, the "Two Jacks"-namely Dyckman,(at the Berkeley Campus in California), and Fisher, (latterly at the Johns Hopkins Campus, in Baltimore), are no longer living, but I am pleased that I knew them, and saw much of them in my Detroit period.

CHAPTER NINETEEN

"My heart's in the Highlands . . ."

"My heart's in the Highlands, my heart is not here;
My heart's in the Highlands a chasing the deer;
A chasing the wild deer, and following the roe,
My heart's in the Highlands, wherever I go.
Farewell to the Highlands, Farewell to the North,
The birth place of Valour, the country of Worth,
Wherever I wander, wherever I rove,
The hills of the Highlands forever I love."

"Farewell to the mountains high cover'd with snow;
Farewell to the straths and green valleys below:
Farewell to the forests and wild hanging woods;
Farewell to the torrents and loud pouring floods.
My heart's in the Highlands, my heart is not here,
My heart's in the Highlands, a chasing the deer:
Chasing the wild deer, and following the roe,
My heart's in the Highlands, wherever I go."

Robert Burns (1759–96)   Source: Rankin,2009.

Though I am a city—boy, Robert Burns' poem here states for me exactly how I have always felt about the Highlands, the place where my heart is, and where my spirit lies. As far back as I can remember in my life, visits to mountains, and to wild places have been both memorable, and important to me. Very early on in life–as a small boy, I can recall being taken on trips from Cardiff to the Brecon Beacons, and 2 other wild places which were not highlands. Thus driving to Ogmore Vale, on what was then a wild part of the Glamorgan Heritage Coast, made a deep impression on me, as did the feeling of freedom and openness when taken on Campbell steamer trips across the vast openness of the Bristol Channel. Later, when being brought up in New Zealand, it was visits to the accessible mountains on the North Island, which were of such importance to me. Going into the Rimutakas, just beyond Wellington Harbour, or up into the Tariruas, when staying at Dannevirke, are glowing highlights in my memories

In adult life, living in Scotland was the best place of all because one had the Pentland Hills on Edinburgh's doorstep, the uplands of the Scottish Borders, and the vast array of mountains and wilderness in the Highlands and Islands to the north and west in Scotland. Work on the Clyde study enabled me to get to know the mountains of the island of Arran, as well as the island of Bute, and parts of upland Argyle. Through my friendship with Prof Sir Robert Grieve, who had been chairman of the Highlands and Islands Development Board, and was the president of the Scottish Mountaineers Club,

Tony climbing on Mt Clisham, on the Isle of Harris,
in the Scottish Outer Hebrides, the UK, 1964

A mid-1930's introduction to the Uplands—my mother and
myself with black berret, (on the left) with the Goodman
family on the Brecon Beacons in South Wales.

there were chances to talk about mountains, and on one occasion–when we were both attending an international conference in the Slovak Tatra Mountains, we were able to go together, albeit by chairlift to the summit of the highest mountain in the chain. My consultancy work with the National Trust for Scotland, created opportunities to get to know parts of the North West of Scotland, and to explore in detail special places like Torridon, the Shetlands, and Rannoch Moor. Work for the Wales Tourist Board enabled me to extend my knowledge and experience of the mountainous uplands in some of the Welsh national parks, and holidays and free time gave chances to explore the uplands of Jura, the Outer Hebrides, the Peak in Hong Kong, and dormant volcanoes in the Canaries.

Work trips also enabled my getting to see and enjoy so many foreign uplands in their national parks, thus the visits to Plitvice Lakes in Croatia, Triglav National Park in Slovenia, Rila and Pirin National Parks in Bulgaria, and on holiday breaks getting to the Italian Dolomites, the New Zealand Southern Alps, as well as to a range of Canadian national parks. There were several dimensions to all of these visits—partly an interest in the effective management of the ecology and wild-life of these habitats, but also a personal need for renewal via the peace, quiet, lack of development, sense of space and fulfillment, found in such places.

I feel a special affinity with writers who have written about Highlands and wild places, with feeling and understanding. Geddes introduced me to the valley profile, coloured by the work of French 19th-century geographers, and giving a feeling of expectation as one moved from Valley settlements and agriculture, into the uplands, with their connotations of wildness, natural vegetation cover, and wildlife. Writers like Wilfred Thessiger shared a sympathy for wild places where the limited populations fitted well ecologically into their habitats. Thus I found I had a natural affinity with the Bedouin who inhabit the Empty Quarter of Arabia, and the Marsh Arabs of

Iraq. Writers like Heinrich Harrer, in his book "Seven years in Tibet" shows a sympathy and sensitivity towards Tibetans living in marginal mountain areas, as well as knowing personally how to survive in demanding Himalayan conditions. Hanbury Tenison's 1984 book also shows this sympathy for indigenous peoples in their habitats, whilst McHarg in his 1971 book showed a professional path forward in such realms, fitting with a" small is beautiful" approach, which was to be developed by Schumacher in 1974.

It is only in the last few years that I have got to know the writings of two British authors–namely Roger Deakin, and Robert Macfarlane, both of whose works give me an enormous sense of joy and fulfilment. In their writings on wilderness—both far and near, plus upon humanised landscapes, they show a level of sympathy and understanding, which is deeply moving. For much of my life I have known and enjoyed the great output in the books of James/Jan Morris, ranging from the Everest expedition, to all the highly perceptive, and deeply sympathetic portraits of port cities–Venice, Sydney, Trieste, and San Francisco. I share with Morris a belief that port cities are especially rich because of the open flows of people, ideas, and goods which characterize such places, compared to closed, introverted, and prejudiced places–which are anathema to me. Other writers, like John Steinbeck, Emile Zola, Brendan Behan, and Fitzroy Maclean give one a sense and range of human insights which one needs both to survive in cities, in wartime and in peace, as well as to know and enjoy—when one is away from people, being in the Highlands, Islands, or in wild places in the lowlands.

There is a particular delight when one is able to enjoy Highlands and wilderness either alone, or with one or two friends with whom one shares values, and a sensitivity to the characteristics of such places. I have enjoyed trips to such places with one or two friends from South Wales, a friend from North Wales, and on other occasions individual friends from the Netherlands, Scotland, or from Norway. There are perhaps two destinations that stay with me as my own special places, one of these is in Scotland, and the other is in Norway. Perhaps on six or seven occasions only, I have spent time in the wild bounds of Knoydart, which is a remote area in the North West of Scotland, where one can walk for 10 or 12 miles without seeing a person, without seeing a road, or buildings, or telegraph posts. Though it is an artificially created wilderness, for historical reasons, it is a place where I find the sense of freedom, openness, joy and calm is unequalled, and therefore very precious. My late Norwegian friend Sondre, introduced me to Hardangervidda,(see Nyquist, 1979), which I have now visited three times, and to which I feel a great sense of connection, sympathy and growing understanding. Perhaps now at the age of 81, on daily dialysis, I will not have further opportunities to visit these two places, but the fact that they are there, known to me and loved by me, give me extra reasons now for the continuity of life, for even their recollection is a source of richness and incredible peace, even when life may be momentarily difficult.

The 1998 visit to South Island, New Zealand, with my wife, gave a series of opportunities not only to see the natural wonders there, but to experience places in ideal conditions. A day of whale-watching at Kaikoura, with Maori guides, a day cruising on the mail boat around the Marlborough Sounds, the trip in the old steamer-the TSS Earnslaw, on Lake Wakatipu, past the Remarkables mountain-range, a sunny day cruising Milford Sound, and as an ultimate—at sunset-landing by helicopter, 8,000 feet up on the Tasman Glacier, where one could stand and watch the sun setting over the 200 mile run of snow-covered Southern Alps, gave one a sense of eternity, perfection, and peace. To have experienced all this with one's wife, both of us in good health, was a pinnacle which one would not want to try and equal.

Bruce Chatwin's writings "In Patagonia," and in his book—"Songlines" about the Australian aborigines, give me a great sense of affinity both with him, and with the peoples about whom he writes. I am fortunate that I have twice had the privilege of getting to know two individuals, who came from unspoiled peoples in wild places. One of these was the Tuareg, about whom I will write in the next chapter, and the other was Ahmad, a Jordanian student whom I first met when lecturing in Rome, and then met twice again when visiting his home near the historic city of Petra, in Jordan. With these two individuals. plus a Negev Bedu whom I met many years ago, have I found an honesty, purity, trustworthiness, and personal sympathy, which I found quite over-whelming. It is the reason why these meetings with just three individuals stay with me all the time. Perhaps what I feel about Highlands, Islands, and wilderness, is remarkably encapsulated in a rare quality that I found in these people, which made me feel that they were not only coloured and shaped by the places they came from, but were perfectly fitted and atuned to their home environments. Just as one may feel that a particular animal species fitted its habitat perfectly, so in these instances one felt there was a wonderful sense of fit between particular human beings and the natural but harsh places, in which they lived.

It is a source of great delight that I find my two sons Theo and Sandy enjoy wild places, and both have an affinity with Highlands and Islands. Sandy's love of mountains has taken him several times to wilderness areas in Alaska, to the mountains of the Himalayas, and to the Andes, as well as to the New Zealand Southern Alps. It gives me much joy that for many years my elder son Theo has taken an annual holiday in the Highlands of Scotland and has rented houses or crofts in winter, to spend time there with his wife and son enjoying the simple pleasures, the space, freedom and quiet of such places. One year when I spent over three weeks teaching a demanding tourism course on the island of Gran Canaria, I found that on a free day I was able to take a country bus, up over the mountain pass, and down into the verdant crater of a great volcano, to the little village of Tejeda.

For a day one could have been almost on another planet, the locals were thoughtful, friendly, and communicative, they spoke a variant on the local patois of Spanish, and almost made one feel like an exotic explorer discovering a new society beyond some rugged boundary, rather like the experience of Ronald Colman, visiting Shangri-La in that extraordinary 1930's film "Lost Horizon". Such brief memorable experiences enrichen life, or as Geddes would have put it "Make life more abundant". Mountains, wilderness, islands, and wild places have made my life more abundant, and whether in student days climbing in the Peak District, or the Lakes, watching the sunset high up in the Southern Alps, or reading books by MacFarlane, or Morris, one sees and knows how incredibly rich the process of living is, and can be.

CHAPTER TWENTY

Tales of a Tuareg Cameleer

Though I have done some three consultancy contracts for the U.N. World Tourism Organisation, namely in the Canaries, in Cyprus, and Algeria—it is in the third instance where the work had the most significant impact, and the most memorable events occurred. This was an extraordinary work contract where the W.T.O. were offering me a modest fee, and expenses, but gave me an extraordinary degree of freedom to shape an international event. The Government of Algeria had asked for an international conference to be held at Tamanrasset, in the mid-Sahara, that would focus on "alternative tourism", and look at ways in which remote rural communities could be empowered to develop sustainable new forms of tourism. Thus I was free to invite world pace-setters in this field, from places as diverse as India and Poland, Wales and Cyprus. What is incredible is that when I tracked down all these remarkable, innovative individuals, and contacted them, they all accepted the invitations to come to an event taking place in the mid-Sahara!

Getting to Southern Algeria was the first challenge! I found it was possible to get a flight from Birmingham to Paris, change planes there, and fly on direct to the city of Algiers, where it was necessary to stay—before one could get an onward flight to Tamanrasset. It took some 2 hours to fly to Paris, and after a wait there, a longer flight across France, and across the Mediterranean to Algiers. I found that city to be an extraordinary place—an exotic mixture of French provincial architecture, and street cafes, fronting an historic kasbah, where the key battle for the end of French colonialism, had taken place. I was accommodated overnight at the Hotel St Georges—an exotic Neo Arabian nights establishment, that made one unsure as to whether you were in Baghdad, or Africa! By day, walking around central Algiers, the mix of European and Islamic Lifestyles was astounding. French style cafes, post offices, and restaurants, contrasted with prayer times, when groups of people would get out of their cars—or stop promenading, to prostate themselves on traffic islands for prayers.

The onward flight to the mid-Sahara proved an even more exotic experience–flying by an old Dakota, with several stops, and a flight time which seemed endless, but must have been only 3 or 4 hours. Most of the flight was over the Sandy Sahara Desert, and the stops were even more exotic–ranging from petroleum extracting plants, to Islamic pilgrimage centres in remote locations. When eventually we did at last arrive in Tamanrasset, there was a decent runway, a modern air terminal, and as the plane landed, Tuareg warriors on camels were firing their guns into the air, and shouting greetings to the visitors! When we left the plane a line of Tuareg musicians were playing a lively welcoming tune for the visitors who had come off the plane. It augured well for the conference, and made me realise in advance, that this was going to be an exceptional place and event. The expected 80 to 100 participants—both international and local, all arrived in the course of 24 hours, many of them being accommodated in a very modest 2 star hotel, the best in town, whilst others were in very basic guesthouses. The conference hall and facilities were good, but there were some major constraints–such as the absence of

International telephone connections, and the very poor quality of the water, which made it necessary to add purification tablets to every drop of water which you drank.

Tony and the Tuareg in the Sahara Desert, at Tamanrasset, in Southern Algeria, 1980's.

On the first evening there was a camel racing event laid on for the visitors, and this was out on the desert edge of the town, where Cameleers raced in the sunset, firing their rifles, whilst their womenfolk in black garb, huddled in groups and ululated hauntingly, whilst the men rode the camels hard. The following morning I went off alone on an exploration of this mid-desert city. It was intriguing to see that the streets had been planted with tamarisk trees, whose deep roots could penetrate down seeking the scarce water resource below. Whilst I was looking at one of these trees, a Tuareg cameleer came up to me and started to talk. At first he spoke what must have been

Berber, then Arabic, but I indicated that I could not understand either of these languages. Then he spoke in French, and at last we were able to converse with each other. He asked me what I was doing and I explained, and then indicated that he was a Cameleer, who was a delegate to our conference, and was in the process of changing over from using camels, to Desert four-wheel drives, and hoped to find a new economic future in eco-tourism, as compared to gun-running, which was one of the past bases for survival! We quickly found that we fully understood each other, using French, and were both keen to continue the conversation. He indicated that he would be here for the whole conference, and was keen to have a daily chat with me, as there was much he wanted to discuss. Thus started one of the most extraordinary contacts of my life, via a set of meetings with this man, with whom I was to have long and memorable conversations in Tamanrasset.

The substantive content of the conference was innovative and significant. We heard how innovators in Indian villages had found ways of creating community-based, Village tourism, which gave employment directly to local people and did not involve international hotel chains at all. Partly meeting the needs of Indian tourists, and partly those of international tourists who were travelling independently, this model showed an effective way forward for alternative tourism, that differed from the norm of international commercial tourism, where the benefits are largely lost to the local host communities. For me, however, it was the set of increasingly long talks between the Tuareg and myself that became the most interesting aspect of my visit. At one stage a German woman reporter who was attending the conference, said to me that she had noticed that I was having these long conversations with a cameleer, and asked if she could take a photo of us together. I said no, I did not want these chats to be disturbed in that way, but unbeknown to me she did later take some shots with a telescopic lens, and then sent them to me in England, for which I was very grateful. What was extraordinary about my conversations with the Tuareg, was how deeply personal they became. He explained about the problems that his mother had, moving from life in a mobile black tent, to living in a rented apartment in the town. This was because the government was trying to urbanise all the Tuaregs, so as to control their activities. His mother found it difficult to switch to this money economy, where you had to pay rent, where you have to pay for electricity, as compared to Desert life, where "the Desert provides all!"

He was also having problems with one of his sons, who did not have an inherited feeling for the freedom of the Desert, and was more attracted to town life, and discos! It was incredible to learn how in a few years the Tuaregs had gone through a process of urbanisation and change, which we in the West had gone through over a much longer period. One day when most of the conference was going out on a day field trip, my Tuareg host asked me not to go, but to join him to go to talk at a cafe out in the desert. That tiny cafe was of camel skins to sit on, with staked Camel skins above, to keep the sun off us, as we sipped glasses of mint-tea. I learned of waterholes in the desert which had dried up, but which years ago had had crocodiles at them, which attracted special birds which ate the insects on their backs. Crocodiles had been shot and disappeared long ago, but the birds still came–looking for them. When it came to parting from the conference, I had my last meeting with the Tuareg, whose name I never learned. I gave him the only gift that I thought would be of any use to him–namely an ex-British Army water carrier, which I brought with me for desert trekking. I thanked him for our conversations, and memorably he said to me "it is not for one man to thank another for something which has greatly enriched them both . . ." With that, he disappeared, and I knew that this would be the last contact we would ever have.

Everything about that visit to Algeria was complex and different. I had promised my wife that I would phone her, to let her know of my safe arrival. When I learnt of the telephone problems in the mid-Sahara, I spoke to an Algerian general who was present at the conference, and he arranged for me to visit an army base nearby, so that I could use the military radio telephone to phone my wife, to say that I'd arrived safely! When I had arrived in Algeria, the customs officer noticed that I had an Israeli Visa in my passport! He said that as I was a guest of the Algerian government, and was there representing the UN, he would cut out the page in my passport with the Israeli Visa, and asked me to hide it away until I had left Algeria! I did this, and had no problems until I arrived at the British customs, who asked me why" I had defaced her Majesty's property!" I explained what had happened in Algeria, which I was told was strictly illegal, and in future I should get a 2nd passport if I was visiting countries that believed the State of Israel does not exist! Whilst the substantive content of the Algerian conference justified it, for me it was this set of meetings with a single Algerian Cameleer which were the highlight of a memorable visit to a place in the heart of the Sahara, where one had meaningful contact with a remarkably thoughtful individual, about all the challenges which were affecting him and his family at that point of time.

The enormous appeal of the Desert—whether the Sahara, the Negev, the Western Desert in Egypt, or the Jordanian Desert setting of Petra, stays with me, and though I can no longer visit such places, their recollection alone is satisfying, and deeply thought-provoking.

CHAPTER TWENTY-ONE

International Tourism Consultancy & Retirement.

At the age of 55 I decided to take early retirement from the University of Birmingham, in order to work independently in the international tourism consultancy field. In my 16 or more years at the University of Birmingham, as a professor heading and directing the Centre for Urban and Regional Studies, my work had included administration, lecturing, tutoring of doctoral students, and quite a lot of consultancy on behalf of the University. Now there was the opportunity to do selective consultancy, either on my own behalf, or in association with major consultancy firms. At first I worked independently and alone, doing such studies as the Tourism Development Action Programme for Cornwall. However, soon I was approached by PIEDA, whose Scottish academic head I knew well, and this quickly led to my involvement in a number of major tourism development studies in Northern Ireland. Of these, the Belfast Tourism Development Strategy was the most significant, and the most enjoyable, as it involved close collaboration with good colleagues, and the opportunity to try out a number of innovative approaches. There was also an exciting opportunity, working for PIEDA, to lead their research team project on behalf of the UK Government to re-examine" Tourism and the Environment". This proved to be a major and fruitful task that resulted in a huge national conference held in London, and leading to the publication of a range of major reports. My work with PIEDA must have lasted about 2 or 3 years, by which time I found I was getting too extensively involved, and needed to leave them.

It's important to remember that as early in my career as 1969/70 I had been involved in tourism consultancy, when we had set up a team to do the Clyde Study. Later there were major studies both for the Scottish Tourist Board, and others for the Wales Tourist Board. The three contracts for the World Tourism Organisation took me to Algeria, to Cyprus, and to the Canaries. As I've indicated earlier in the text, work for bodies such as the UK Know-How Fund had led to my work in Bulgaria, projects for the Pacific Area Travel Association resulted in my consultancy work in both Hong Kong, and the Maldives, whilst work later for the United Nations Priority Actions Programme had led to work tasks in Albania, and in Cyprus. When I had taken early retirement and was free to select which consultancy I wanted to do, I joined some Irish colleagues whose firm was contracted to do a range of studies on the Glendalough National Park, in Ireland, and that consultancy was both extremely interesting, the colleagues with whom I worked were stimulating, and the National Park itself a great pleasure both to work upon and in. In the post-university period, time was available to participate in events such as the World Travel Market in London, and the International Tourist Mart (ITB), in Berlin. Work with the Dublin consultancy led to some unusual tasks on behalf of Irish clients, such as examining and evaluating the new phase of" Health, Wellness, and Well-being Tourism" which was developing rapidly in Switzerland, France, Hungary, Germany, and Austria. This is all indicative of the wide and stimulating range of work abroad in which I was able to get involved after the age of 55.

My professional work over the last 50 years has not only given me strong links with the Royal Town Planning Institute, and the Tourism Society, but has led to my very active involvement in three international associations. These are AIEST—the International Association of Scientific Experts in Tourism, JHUF—the Johns Hopkins University Urban Fellows Association, and TRC–the Tourist Research Centre, an essentially Europe-wide network. My deep involvement in AIEST led to my becoming a member of its international executive, and attending some 8 of its annual conferences–held in Italy, Holland, Hungary, Croatia, France, Austria, Germany, and Switzerland. Through the JHUF, which for 4 years I chaired, there were some 11 annual conferences which I attended, and these were held in Yugoslavia, France, the UK, Romania, the Netherlands, Poland, Italy, Bulgaria, the USA, and Croatia. Thus through consultancy on the one hand, lecturing invitations abroad, and my involvement with these three international associations, my travel has been frequent and extensive, but much of it has been focused upon European destinations. Jointly chairing a project for the Vienna Social Science Research Centre, involved participants from six European nations, and led to more European travel, as did my attendance and participation at two Chamonix-Mont Blanc summits–which were worthwhile Franco-Swiss conferences held in the ski-resort of Chamonix.

In the 1990's, as I have already mentioned earlier in the book, I was invited by a major Spanish consultancy, to work on their behalf, directing a major E.U. two-year project in Poland. This was the largest consultancy task which I undertook in the period of my so-called" early retirement", and it was the most difficult and demanding task of all. The complexity of the management system, the inadequate communications within the structure of the European Union's bureaucracy, the differing aims in Brussels of the European Union, to those of the Consultants in Barcelona, and of the clients in Warsaw, plus the impossible expectations on the part of the Poles, lead to results which could not possibly satisfy everybody. I had taken on this task when I was 60 years old, and as indicated earlier–it destroyed my health, and lead to my hospital treatment in Lodz. Perhaps it was wiser that by the time I was in my 70's I had decided not to do any more consultancy, but to concentrate on writing, and the occasional lecture. From the age of 75 to 79, I was working on my first major textbook for C.A.B.I. publishers in England, and that book was published and launched when I was 79 years old. By then I had been seeing a renal consultant at a local hospital for about 10 years, as my kidneys had been steadily declining in their function, and so in the year 2011 I had to start on kidney dialysis, which I have now been doing for over one and a half years. Because I opted for peritoneal dialysis, it is necessary to do this at home some 4 times a day, so in effect this ended my frequent International travel, and obliged me to live within much smaller geographical boundaries. Thus my wife and I have taken trying to do a 15 minute walk daily, and this has encouraged us to optimise

International Connections: Tony speaking at the Chamonix Summit Conference, Hosting the Johns Hopkins Conference in Birmingham, and attending the Urban Fellows Conference in Lille, France.

upon local opportunities that exist–such as walkingin the Birmingham Botanical Gardens, in the Vale residential site of the University of Birmingham, with its large lake, and the Winterbourne site, which includes a fine arts and crafts house, which has a museum, café, has gardens, and an adjacent nature reserve, with its large lake and bird-life. The richness of this green environment—all within about 5 minutes of our house, makes me appreciate how privileged we are to live in such an advantaged location in a large British city.

The work on this current book–which is my second book, is part of the range of things which I am now fortunate enough to be doing in my 81st year. The extraordinary range of human contacts made through my teaching, international consultancy and travel, gives me a great richness of human contacts, which are rewarding in this period of my real retirement, so to speak, and the range of correspondence, phone calls and e-mails, is supplemented by the valued visits from my family on the one hand, and from friends on the other hand–who come here on visits from Australia, the USA, Greece, Scotland, Denmark, Slovenia, Poland, Holland, and Switzerland. This makes one continue to feel that you remain part of the global village, even if constraining personal health circumstances may limit one's international travel.

Personally guiding over 30 doctoral students on their successful theses has been a special privilege, as one enjoys a rare intellectual intimacy with others when doing such tutoring! In the course of my working life I have published over 300 reports, articles, papers and lectures, in addition to my 2 books, so I feel that there is some continuing contribution in this way. My hero–Professor Patrick Geddes, produced one major book, contributed to 3 or 4 others, produced several important technical reports, but it was his extraordinary lecturing involvement that directly affected so many people. My own range of lectures in many different locations will have—I hope served the purpose of stimulating and informing others, but I hope my written output may be a long life contribution in the three fields which have been so important to me, namely town planning, tourism—and leisure-services planning, plus tourism planning education. It has been a long, rewarding, and fulfilling life, and for that I am deeply grateful. My wife and family have been the anchor for me in a mobile life, where the whole world has been my canvas, to explore!

APPENDIX A

Bibliography

Abercrombie, Patrick.(with JH Forshaw) 1943 The County of London Plan.

Abercrombie, Patrick 1944 The Greater London Plan.

Affolter.Michael.T.1973. Rural Resource Planning: Towards an Operational Framework. 2 vols. Ph D Thesis. E.C.A.& Heriot Watt University, Edinburgh.

Armstrong. James.L. 1984. Contemporary Prestige Centres for Art,& Culture, Exhibitions, Sports & Conferences: An International Survey. Ph D Thesis. University of Birmingham.

Behan.Brendan 1958 Borstal Boy. Hutchinson, London

Barbellion.WNP 1948 The Journal of a Disappointed Man. Penguin.

Burbridge.Veronica.1973 . Rural Resource Potential: an Examination of Land capability analysis in rural planning. PhD thesis, ECA & Heriot Watt University, Edinburgh.

Chapman.JM and Brian.1957.The Life and Times of Baron Haussmann.Weidenfeld and Nicolson.

Chatwin.Bruce 1987. The Songlines. Vintage Classics

Chatwin.Bruce 1988. In Patagonia. Vintage Classics.

Collins English Dictionary

Deakin. Roger. 2000 Waterlog-A Swimmer's journey through Britain. Vintage.

Deakin.Roger 2007 .Wildwood—A Journey Through Trees. Free Press.

Drummond. Maldwin.1996. John Bute-An Informal Portrait. Michael Russell.

Eniola. Mubo A.1987. Planning for Tourism in Kwara State (Nigeria)-A realistic and result-based approach. PhD thesis, University of Birmingham.

Fuks, Hoffman et al . undated/circa 1982 Polnische Juden-Geschichte und Kultur. Verlag Interpress.

Geddes.Patrick 1949 Reprint. Cities in Evolution. Williams & Norgate. London.

Geddes.Patrick 1904. City Development-A Study of Parks, Gardens,& Culture Institutes.St George Press. Birmingham.

Geddes.Patrick 1921 Town Expansion Plan for Tel Aviv. Unpublished Report.

Hamesse.jean-Elie. 1998. Gartengestaltung mit Altmaterial: praktische andwendungen fur eine wirtschaftliche und okologische Nutzung. Deutche Verlags-Anstalt. Stuttgart.

Hanbury-Tenison. Robin.1984. Worlds Apart—An Explorer's Life. Granada.

Harrer.Heinrich 1994 Seven Years in Tibet. Flamingo.

Hawkins-Ferry .W. 1968. The Buildings of Detroit-A History. Wayne State University Press. Detroit.

Hemingway.E. 1929. Farewell to Arms. Scribner & Sons. New York.

Hibberd.Dominic.2003. Wilfrid Owen—A New Biography. Phoenix.

Holliday.John 1997 Letters from Jerusalem during the Palestine Mandate/Eunice Holliday. Radcliffe Press.

Huxley. A. 1932. Brave New World. Chatto & Windus.

Jenkins. Ian.S,2007. Postmodern Tourism Niches: UK Literary Festivals & their importance for Tourism Destination Development. PhD thesis. University of Swansea.

Kaikis.Z. 2007. Feasibility for Development of new rural accommodation establishments in the province of Kalampaka (Greece). M.Sc Thesis, Coll. of Food/University of Birmingham.

Karpowicz.Z.J. 1987. The Polish Park System. Ph D thesis. The University of Birmingham.

Koestler. A. 1960 (reprint) Thieves in the Night. Panther Books.

Koscak. M. 1992. Integrated Rural Development. PhD thesis. University of Ljubljana, Slovenia.

Lewis. Sinclair 1920. Main Street. Harcourt, Brace & House.

Libaek & Stenersen .1995. A History of Norway. Grondalog Dreyers Forlag AS, Oslo.

Lowdermilk WC.1946 Palestine-Land of Promise.Victor Gollancz.Ltd.

Lyon.D. 2001 Le Corbusier alive. Editions Pierre Terrail.

Mc Dowall. D. 2010. Bute. The Laird Press, Richmond, Surrey.

Macfarlane. Robert .2007 .The Wild Places. Granta

Macfarlane. Robert. 2003 Mountains of the Mind. Granta

McHarg. Ian 1971. Design with Nature. Doubleday

Mairet. P.1957.Pioneer of Sociology-Life & Letters of P.Geddes. Lund Humphries.

Martin. John R. 2003 Rongotai—A History of Rongotai College 1928-2003, Rongotai College Old Boys Association.

Massana. Juan, del Castillo,2003.Catedrales del Agua. Ollero y Ramos Editores

Mazower. Mark. 2004. Salonica-City of Ghosts. Harper Perennial.

Morris. J .1960 Venice. Faber

Morris. J. 1993 Hong Kong—Epilogue to an Empire. Penguin.

Morris. J .1993. Sydney. Penguin

Morris J. 2003 Coronation Everest. Faber & Faber

Mumford. Lewis.1934.Technics & Civilisation. Harcourt Brace.New York

Mumford. Lewis.1938.The Culture of Cities. Harcourt Brace. New York.

Murray. WH. 1966. The Hebrides. William Heinemann, London.

Newcastle upon Tyne City Planning Dept. 196? First Review of the City Development Plan.

Nyquist. FP. 1979. Hardangervidda. Grondal & Son Forlag.AS. Oslo.

OECD.1980.The Impact of Tourism upon the Environment. OECD. Paris.

Ombler.K. 1999. Wellington and Beyond. New Holland Publishers (NZ) Ltd.

Papageorgiou, Fouli.1978.The Cognitive Components of Leisure Mentality etc. PhD Thesis, University of Birmingham.

PAP/RAC 2003 .Guide to Good Practice in Tourism Carrying Capacity Assessment. PAP/RAC. Split, Croatia.

PATA,1983.International Workshop for Pacific Nations, on Tourism Impacts. Hong Kong.

Pearson, Cowburn & Travis.1951-4. '244' University of Manchester.

Prieto-Moreno.F.1983. Los Jardines de Granada. Ministerio de Education y Ciencia. ERISA/GREPOL. Madrid.

Rankin.Ian. 2009 The Poems of Robert Burns. Penguin.

Robinson-William.1869. The Parks, Promenades & Gardens of Paris.. John Murray.

Samuel.Edwin.1970 A Lifetime in Jerusalem. Vallentine Mitchell.

Schumacher.E.F. 1974 Small is Beautiful—A Study of Economics as if People Mattered. Abacus.

Segev, Tom . 2000 One Palestine, Complete-Jews & Arabs under the British Mandate. Little, Brown, and Co.

Steinbeck.J. 1939 The Grapes of Wrath. Viking. New York.

Steinbeck..J. 1949 Of Mice and Men. Penguin.

Stendhal . 1953 Scarlet and Black. Penguin Books. London

Stewart. Graham .2010 Wellington-The Best Little Capital City in the World Grantham House Publishing.NZ.

Sykes.Christopher 1959 Orde Wingate Collins. London.

Thessiger.W. 1964 Arabian sands. Penguin Travel Library

Thessiger.W. 1964 Marsh Arabs Penguin Travel Library

Towner.John.1984. The European Grand Tour, circa 1550-1840: A Study of its role in the History of Tourism. PhD Thesis, 2Vols. University of Birmingham.

Travis.A.S. 1970 Recreation Planning for the Clyde. Scottish Tourist Board, Edinburgh.

Travis.A.S. 1984. Realising the Tourist potential of the South Wales Valleys. The Wales Tourist Board, Cardiff.

Travis.A.S. 1986. Study of the Social, Cultural & Linguistic Impacts of Tourism in and upon Wales. 2 vols. ECTARC & Wales Tourist Board.

Travis A.S. 1991 New Tourism Trends & New Tourism Products. 26 Nation Seminar report, Nicosia, Cyprus. World Tourist Organisation, Madrid.

Travis.A.S.et al 2000 New Synagogue Siting, Design, and Development-

Towards Sustainability. Report to the BoD of BJ.

Travis.A.S. 2011 Planning for Tourism, Leisure & Sustainability. CABI, UK.

Van Egmond .T.2007. Understanding Western Tourists in Developing Countries. CABI. Wallingford Oxon.UK.

Vinecour.Earl. 1977 Polish Jews: The Last Chapter. New York University Press.

Webber, J. 2009. Rediscovering Traces of Memory: The Jewish Heritage of Polish Galicia. Littman Library/Indiana University Press.

Werth.A. 1939. France and Munich. Hamilton.

Werth.A. 1946. The Year of Stalingrad. Hamilton.

Werth.A. 1956. France 1940-1955. Robert Hale.

Werth.A. 1957.The Strange History of Pierre Mendes-France & The Great Conflict over French North Africa. Barrie.

Willmott. and Young 195? Family and Kinship in East London. Penguin.

Ziberna.Marjan 2008 Dolenjska-The Rolling Hills of Slovenia.Zalozba Goga.

Zola.Emile. 1954 Edition. Germinal. Penguin Books.

APPENDIX B

Family Trees

The Tavrogis Family Tree

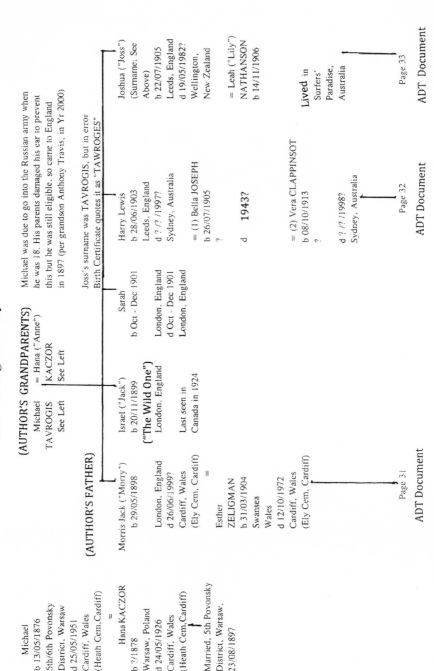

Michael was due to go into the Russian army when he was 18. His parents damaged his ear to prevent this but he was still eligible, so came to England in 1897 (per grandson Anthony Travis, in Yr 2000)

Joss's surname was TAVROGIS, but in error Birth Certificate quotes it as "TAWROGES"

(AUTHOR'S GRANDPARENTS)

Michael = Hana ("Anne")
TAVROGIS   KACZOR
See Left   See Left

Michael
b 13/05/1876
5th/6th Povonsky District, Warsaw
d 25/05/1951
Cardiff, Wales
(Heath Cem, Cardiff)
=
Hana KACZOR
b ?/1878
Warsaw, Poland
d 24/05/1926
Cardiff, Wales
(Heath Cem, Cardiff)
Married, 5th Povonsky District, Warsaw, 23/08/1897

(AUTHOR'S FATHER)

Morris Jack ("Morty")
b 29/05/1898
London, England
d 26/06/1992
Cardiff, Wales
(Ely Cem, Cardiff)
=
Esther
ZELIGMAN
b 31/03/1904
Swansea
Wales
d 12/10/1972
Cardiff, Wales
(Ely Cem, Cardiff)

Israel ("Jack")
b 20/11/1899
["The Wild One"]
London, England

Last seen in Canada in 1924

Sarah
b Oct - Dec 1901
London, England
d Oct - Dec 1901
London, England

Harry Lewis
b 28/06/1903
Leeds, England
d ?, ?, /1997?
Sydney, Australia

= (1) Bella JOSEPH
b 26/07/1905
?

d   1943?

= (2) Vera CLAPPINSOT
b 08/10/1913
?

d ?, ?, /1998?
Sydney, Australia

Joshua ("Joss")
(Surname: See Above)
b 22/07/1905
Leeds, England
d 19/05/1982?
Wellington, New Zealand

= Leah ("Lily")
NATHANSON
b 14/11/1906

Lived in Surfers' Paradise, Australia

Page 31

ADT Document

Page 32

ADT Document

Page 33

ADT Document

The Tavrogis Family Tree

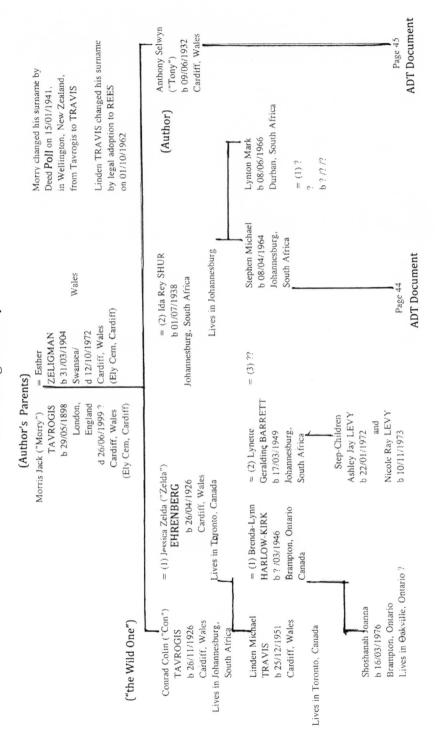

(Author's Parents)

Morris Jack ("Morry")
TAVROGIS
b 29/05/1898
London,
England
d 26/06/1999 ?
Cardiff, Wales
(Ely Cem, Cardiff)

= Esther
ZELIGMAN
b 31/03/1904
Swansea/
d 12/10/1972
Cardiff, Wales
(Ely Cem, Cardiff)

Wales

Morry changed his surname by
Deed Poll on 15/01/1941,
in Wellington, New Zealand,
from Tavrogis to TRAVIS

Linden TRAVIS changed his surname
by legal adoption to REES
on 01/10/1962

= (2) Ida Rey SHUR
b 01/07/1938
Johannesburg, South Africa

Lives in Johannesburg

(Author)

Anthony Selwyn
("Tony")
b 09/06/1932
Cardiff, Wales

Page 45

ADT Document

("the Wild One")

Conrad Colin ("Con")
TAVROGIS
b 26/11/1926
Cardiff, Wales

Lives in Johannesburg,
South Africa

= (1) Jessica Zelda ("Zelda")
EHRENBERG
b 26/04/1926
Cardiff, Wales

Lives in Toronto, Canada

= (3) ??

Step-Children
Ashley Jay LEVY
b 22/01/1972
and
Nicole Ray LEVY
b 10/11/1973

Lynton Mark
b 08/06/1966
Durban, South Africa

Stephen Michael
b 08/04/1964
Johannesburg,
South Africa

= (1) ?
?
b ? ? /?

Page 44

ADT Document

Linden Michael
TRAVIS
b 25/12/1951
Cardiff, Wales

= (1) Brenda-Lynn
HARLOW-KIRK
b ? /03/1946
Brampton, Ontario
Canada

= (2) Lynette
Geraldine BARRETT
b 17/03/1949
Johannesburg,
South Africa

Lives in Toronto, Canada

Shoshanah Joanna
b 16/03/1976
Brampton, Ontario
Lives in Oakville, Ontario ?

The Tavrogis Family Tree

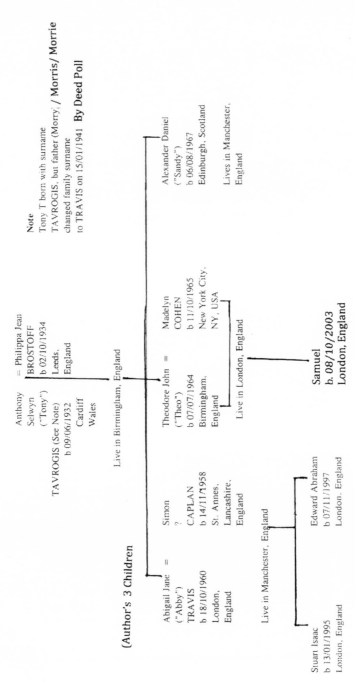

Note

Tony T born with surname
TAVROGIS, but father (Morry) / **Morris / Morrie**
changed family surname
to TRAVIS on 15/01/1941 **By Deed Poll**

Anthony
Selwyn
("Tony")
TAVROGIS (See Note)
b 09/06/1932
Cardiff
Wales

== Philippa Jean
BROSTOFF
b 02/10/1934
Leeds,
England

Live in Birmingham, England

(Author's 3 Children)

Abigail Jane =
("Abby")
TRAVIS
b 18/10/1960
London,
England

Simon
?
CAPLAN
b 14/11/1958
St. Annes.
Lancashire,
England

Live in Manchester, England

Theodore John =
("Theo")
b 07/07/1964
Birmingham,
England

Madelyn
COHEN
b 11/10/1965
New York City.
NY, USA

Live in London, England

Alexander Daniel
("Sandy")
b 06/08/1967
Edinburgh. Scotland

Lives in Manchester,
England

Stuart Isaac
b 13/01/1995
London, England

Edward Abraham
b 07/11/1997
London. England

Live in Manchester, England

Samuel
b. 08/10/2003
London, England

(Author's 3 Grandsons)

Lightning Source UK Ltd.
Milton Keynes UK
UKOW041937100513

210513UK00001B/48/P